Warrior Of Light : Stories of Life + Death

Karyn Crisis

Copyright © 2021 Karyn Crisis. All rights reserved.

Front cover photo: Bonnie Rae Mills, Copyright © 2011
Back cover photo: Davide Tiso, Copyright © 2015

Copyright: Golden Bough Books, 2021

ISBN: 978-0-578-99689-9

Warrior Of Light : Stories of Life + Death

1. Levitation .... Page 5
2. Death + Resurrection .... Page 9
3. Love Heals .... Page 15
4. Over My Body .... Page 17
5. Triplicate .... Page 19
6. Flying Indoors .... Page 21
7. Night Gatherings .... Page 23
8. Iron Lady .... Page 27
9. Seeing The Future .... Page 31
10. Ghosted .... Page 33
11. Ocean Omphalos .... Page 35
12. Fire In The Night .... Page 39
13. Angels In The Darkness .... Page 43
14. Wisdom Of My Violin .... Page 47
15. I Heard It From The Trees .... Page 51
16. The Saving Grace Of Disembodied Voices .... Page 53
17. Time Jump .... Page 57
18. Dating In The Twilight Zone .... Page 59
19. Entranced .... Page 61
20. Winged .... Page 67
21. Art In The Air .... Page 69
22. Golden White Light Of Death .... Page 73
23. Out With The Old, In With The New .... Page 77
24. Dreaming Of What's To Come .... Page 79
25. Feeling Others .... Page 83
26. Tuxedo .... Page 85
27. Remote View .... Page 89
28. Playing With Time .... Page 91
29. My Man Voice .... Page 93
30. Estate Sale .... Page 97
31. New Year's Death .... Page 101
32. Witch Hunt .... Page 103
33. Surrender To The Unknown .... Page 107
34. Ghosts V Guides .... Page 109
35. Creepythings .... Page 113
36. Double Trouble .... Page 117
37. Freak Magnet .... Page 121
38. Conduit .... Page 125
39. Hotel Intruder .... Page 127
40. Initiation .... Page 129
41. Tarot .... Page 133
42. Summoning .... Page 135
43. Catching Thieves .... Page 137
44. Shape Shifting .... Page 139
45. Soul Retrieval .... Page 141
46. Continuity .... Page 145

This is a small collection of stories from the time period of my birth to 2009 ish.

They are stories of life and death I can offer from my life as a naturally developing psychic, spirit Medium, artist and musician.

They are the foundation of what came after.

After 2009 I trained as a Spiritualist Medium, then my life took on a decidedly specific path towards rural Italian traditions, reclaiming feminine magic and pre-Roman Divine Feminine history, which you can read more about in these books:

"Italy's Witches and Medicine Women Vol 1"
"Italian Magic : Secret Lives Of Women"

To learn more about your own spiritual abilities you may want to visit my online Golden Bough School at: www.karyncrisisheals.com

LEVITATION

It was 7:30 pm, May 2012, and I had decided to take a break from painting. I had been oil painting for 10 hours a day every day for 2 months in preparation for my upcoming solo gallery show. The show's theme was the Major Arcana of the Tarot, in 21 oil paintings. I'd also built from scratch the 21 stretched canvases in custom sizes that I'd been painting on. Since I had to spend so many continuous hours just sitting and painting in order to complete this body of work, whenever I had to run an errand I would lightly jog on my way there and back in order to get some exercise.

On this Friday eve, there was still plenty of gorgeous San Francisco sunlight, and I put on my ipod at a low volume and began to lightly jog down my side street towards an intersection with a major avenue: Geary Avenue. At this time of day, there was hardly any car or foot traffic, but instead a peaceful lull. I was enjoying the fresh air and the wind. There was always wind in this neighborhood of San Francisco, in fact whatever direction I'd walk in, I was always against the wind.

I was enjoying the beautiful quality of light. The sun seemed to just be setting so the light was golden, and even the air felt golden. There was a quiet, still, dreamy atmosphere. I seemed to be the only one out and about. I jogged to the corner of St. Joseph's Avenue and Geary, a wide-open corner where I had a very clear view of the downward sloping Geary Boulevard and the cross street I was moving towards. Geary was a long main 2-way road running from one side of San Francisco to the other, and even though it was usually packed with traffic, there were times during the day and night where there were lulls in traffic and this was one of them. Behind me was Kaiser Hospital. This part of the corner on my left had a lot of visibility, firstly because it was a wide-rounded corner rather than a right angle, and secondly because it served as a drop-off and load-up area for visitors and patients to the hospital and so it was much larger than an average street corner. The rounded sidewalk was big enough to host a small farmer's market once a week. The speed limit was only 35 mph and yet it wasn't really adhered to by drivers.

As I jogged to the curb, I saw not a a single car in sight, nor any pedestrians, which was a little odd, and I noticed the light turned green. I felt myself jog forward and my right foot touch the street, and even though I still felt like I was jogging forwards, suddenly I was aware of my entire body being lifted up, moved backwards, and somehow I was back up on the curb and then moved even further back, a few feet before the curb, as both of my feet made gentle contact with the sidewalk.

Time suddenly suspended, in the way scenes freeze yet keep moving in the Matrix movies, and I realized even though I was moving my body forwards, something or someone else was moving me backwards, but before I could think about this, and as soon as I was on the curb, a speeding car came blazing downhill out of nowhere, much faster than the 35 mph speed limit, and it careened across the curb edge where I would've been, as it rounded the corner, screeching loudly.

As time seemed to both slow down yet maintain its real-life pace, I saw a vision of my own body fly up into the sky in a slowly rotating ball. I could see the bottoms of my black-soled Vans sneakers, my legs curled against my butt and the backside of my hair, which was curled around my back and flew away just where my hips were. I could see my shoulders and how small they seemed, and the back of my head, and I was touched at how small and fragile I looked, almost like a child curled up into a ball, way up in the air. It brought tears to my eyes, seeing myself in this compassionate way, oddly gracefully floating up in the air and slowly rotating in an elegant half-time speed from what would have been the impact of the car hitting me. It was a poetic and endearing moment, watching myself from the outside, aware of my physical fragility, and it somehow caused me to appreciate all my little body has endured in this life.

Simultaneously I saw the car, in an even more slowed-down motion, whose driver was looking to the left, instead of at me and where she was turning (to the right). I was struck by her beauty-she reminded me of a particular famous model. I could see how smooth her skin was against her cheekbones, the way the light glistened against her skin. She was thin and must have been tall as well, because the driver's seat was pushed back quite far, much further back than the passenger seat, and just her fingertips were on the wheel of the car. Where the sun touched her skin, golden and caramel tones seemed to glisten in the light. Her hair was pulled up into a high bun, and her eyes were intense and fixed. Her body in contrast seemed so relaxed and calmly focused on speeding full throttle around the corner. She never once looked in my direction.

Her car was a beige cadillac with cream colored fabric seats and it too was filled with the golden light of the hour. I also saw, as she blasted over the corner where I would've been, gunning away at lightning speed, a possible future for her having killed another pedestrian a few blocks away and having been arrested and put in jail.

In this vision, her beauty looked strange in contrast to the prison outfit, and I felt my heart ache for her possible future and for the person she killed. I was surprised to be so full of emotions and feelings for someone I'd not even met and something that hadn't actually occurred. Then, suddenly real time seemed to snap back, and the light was green and the street was clear, and I found myself calmly jogging across the street as if I'd never even stopped running, smiling and feeling grateful to be alive. I didn't even have the time to be angry at her, I was overwhelmed by the compassion I felt for both of us in that strange predicament, and I was grateful to see what could have been but was not. Perhaps even stranger was that I felt myself able to shake off this entire experience without even trying.

=

This experience of being physically levitated and of perceiving time and space through multiple perspectives simultaneously is an example of how Source can move us beyond what we perceive as limitations: I can't repeat this set of conditions all by myself. I can try to think my way here again, but I'm not able to move into this experience on my own.

It's also a demonstration how holding a positive mood can benefit us in ways we can't necessarily predict: because events are always unfolding around us, our mood and attitude can move us closer or farther away from situations that we may judge as good or bad but really just match our emotions. It's possible that had I gone jogging in an impatient mood, I might have been far less relaxed and in-the-flow, which could have resulted in me determining to get my errand done as fast as possible, pushing my will no matter what, and therefore rushing across the street and getting hit, desiring to be fixed in my mood, just like the driver. Instead I was very open during that time, feeling appreciation for the celestial atmosphere of the day and the beauty of just being alive in that moment, in which I surrendered to the time-suspended, dreamy kind of experience.

I try to make this choice when I perceive tension in myself and out in society. For example, when at the airport, which I've used frequently, I'd just surrender my place in line if there was an aggressive person next to me. If I'd be driving somewhere and noticed a road rager behind me, I give them all the space they need, pulling to the side if I need to, allowing them to zoom along. If a cashier is in a bad mood and dumping it on me and kind or lighthearted words from me don't lift the vibe, I take my checkout basket to another line.

I make the decision in a moment to just give up the stress to whomever wants it, and I step to the side. I choose to enjoy myself and not be infected by someone else's emotions. Before going out in public I also do energy work on myself so my environment matches my vibe when I step into the world, which may require me to be fully aware of my bad moods and to keep them to myself and allow myself to process them without affecting others. If I do come across something that's not enjoyable and if it's also not necessary for me to stand my ground, I just step to the side. I call it "stepping out of society".

More importantly, these moments are a call to attention, asking me to adjust myself, showing me how I'm a match for something in that undesirable experience. If I'm fast enough to acknowledge this, take responsibility, and to then choose to change my vibe into something I prefer fast enough, I can be that vibration I prefer, and co-create that vibe around me.

DEATH + RESURRECTION

The first time I died I was 12 years old.

My mother had driven my sister and I down to visit our godparents in the summer, 1980s ish. They loved to cook and, having arrived late at night after a full day's drive, presented us with us a huge dinner. Desert was a simple vanilla ice cream with just a few ingredients and contained nothing I was allergic to, a rarity. I had a small bite when I felt my throat immediately start to constrict as is typical of anaphylactic shock, a potentially deadly allergic reaction I'd experienced before. My mother tried to figure out how I was allergic to that ice cream, considering both she and my godmother scoured those 5 ingredients over and over again. No one had yet suspected instead the new medicine my doctor had prescribed (a specific antibiotic). The adults were getting involved in a heated discussion, and I needed to be alone to try and slow down this reaction in my body which was rapidly becoming urgent. I left the dining room to be alone in the darkened other rooms of their enormous house to sense more clearly what was going on in my body, and I made my way up the giant wooden staircase upstairs, which was in total darkness.

I remember my throat was closing down even more and I was becoming dizzy as I reached the top of the staircase and walked past the main room with the two child ghosts I didn't like. Slowly, because even at this young age I had so much experience with my body being in urgent situations that in this particular case I was well aware I needed to keep my heart rate down by being calm.

Suddenly all the other ghosts from the other rooms gathered in the hallway which made it even more horrible. They were not nice ghosts. I was beginning to lose consciousness so instead of closing myself in the bathroom like I wanted to, also because there were two mean child ghosts in there, I decided I had to return to the adults. This was a difficult decision for me because I didn't trust any adults with my body or my life at this point (having been poked and prodded and experimented on since my earliest days on earth) but I was sure I'd die if I didn't immediately go downstairs.

During anaphylactic shock, small blood vessels in the body begin to leak blood into the body's tissues. This can cause a sudden and dramatic drop in blood pressure, which is why I was becoming so dizzy. Asphyxia can occur due to airways suddenly seizing and restricting oxygen to the lungs, and cardiovascular shock can occur due to sudden drop in blood pressure which prevents the heart from getting enough oxygen. I was struggling to breathe and stay conscious.

Anyone in anaphylaxis shock can die within 15 minutes. I didn't know all these details at the time, but I'd been through this before and could feel in my own body the terrifying urgency: throat closing, eyelids swelling shut, lips swelling so much they turn inside-out, and the biggest part of it: feeling like some giant hand is squeezing my throat closed and squeezing my heart until the pressure makes me feel like I'll both explode and pass out. I knew my life was at stake.

I don't remember how I got myself downstairs, I just remember things becoming blurry and going dark with the sounds of adults panicking around me, yelling instructions to each other. Then I remember being in the front seat of a car between my mom and godfather as he was trying to start the car, wondering how late it was...midnight? So dark. My godfather (who was a psychiatrist and had medical training) was shouting at my mom that she needed to slap me to keep me awake, that they couldn't let me go to sleep…something about me going into shock.

And then…I remember some flashes of consciousness where it felt like I was lying down, looking at a deep red painted brick wall with a bright light above me as I woke up attached to a heart monitor, my mother helping me pee in one of those kidney shaped metal trays, then darkness again.

I awoke again surrounded by those deep red painted bricks, and I noticed they were the walls of a square emergency room. I was on a metal operating table in the middle of this room with a large, blinding bright light above me. It almost felt like a loading zone in a warehouse. The door, though closed, was as wide as the wall itself. A handsome doctor with dark hair was leaning on one arm dangling heart monitor suction cups and their connective wires over me with a swagger, asking me if I wanted to keep them as a souvenir. He congratulated me on surviving, and he said he was impressed. He told me they'd lost me but brought me back, and he was quite proud of that.

I played cool and pretended I was fine even though at this moment I couldn't feel most of my body and had no idea how many hours it had been. Being that I felt like an adult trapped in a child's body during my childhood, I felt this need to always be strong and pretend everything was under control, so I shrugged it all off like a typical day of battle and of course I didn't take the heart monitor cups that had brought me back to life. I don't remember leaving that place.

Everything went black again. I remember waking up hazily in my godparents' room on the ground floor. They and my mom were on the edge of the bed I was in, watching an art film. They seemed so far away. To the left was a glass wall with a view to the lush grassy backyard. Apparently I was in that bed in that room for 2 weeks.

People always ask me what it was like to be dead, but I can't remember. Years later I'd die again and remember everything. This time though, it was dark and I was in-and-out of consciousness.

I only remember what it was like to be alive after dying: ghosts were even more present in my life than they already were, premonitions were more frequent, I could intuitively read adults and know who was lying (and I was never wrong when it came to authority figures), I predicted much of my own life, felt little separation between me and the spirit world even though I didn't know what to do with this…it was just that life was more crowded and I often spoke out loud to people no one else could see, and my classmates seemed to feel comfortable confiding their deepest fears and secrets in me, which looked like the most popular kids inviting me to spend time at their houses, whereas before they made fun of me or bullied me. For a while, the angels I knew since earlier years seemed to fade into the background. But this was mostly how I already lived life.

Perhaps most dramatic change was the arrival of a new "friend" I gained from this experience: a spirit I called the "angel of death", a figure I didn't believe in before. I wasn't scared of him, I considered him someone who was challenging me. He had a face like a skull, very cliche, and he did wear a black cloak. As much as I thought I was imagining him, I couldn't erase him nor rid my ears of his goading laughter.

I'd come to know him well, for the next 10 years or so after I'd leave Chicago area and move to Manhattan, where I'd have to get myself through asthma attacks without medicine. I'd learned that going to the emergency room often worsened my lungs because they would just pump me up with too much of the steroid inhaler medicine which would make me faint. Then, they'd send me home and not even 30 minutes later I'd be having asthma attacks again, for hours, and have to cure myself all over again.

So, during these times of asthma attacks, I would instead lock myself in the bathroom. The angel of death would always be on my left side, right next to my face, laughing at me and trying to goad me into giving up while I cared for myself which involved, through all the gasping for air and drooling spittle, training myself to try and slow down my breathing and my heart rate.

And at a certain point, all the muscles in my back, abdomen and all the strength in my lungs simply can't work anymore: they freeze in pain (or lack of oxygen) and there's a risk that the heart will stop. It's not just that breathing isn't possible…it's that the lungs don't expand or expel, so there's not the ability to breathe in and out as normal, and on top of that the entire body goes into emergency and works so very hard that it loses its ability to do what it does.

The extreme exhaustion all my muscles felt in these moments made it that much harder to just sit up and fight this battle. Muscles working overdrive meant they would freeze/burn locked into place. Lying down meant I couldn't breathe at all. So at this point was when I would often pass out..and fortunately I'd always come to again.

I saw my life flash before my eyes too, in the way "they" say it does, watching a movie review of my life of how I'd affected everyone I had met.

I became a warrior during those battles between my lungs and the angel of death. I always told him to fuck off and it was always a competition I refused to lose, partly just because he was a man and since I was born men were trying to limit me or harm me, partly because I'd been taught by adults since my earliest age that no one would help me in any situation. It was up to me to help myself.

At some point in my life, this angel of death gave up and departed. The asthma attacks did too.

Years later, during a visit with my mother, she started recounting that time. For some reason my family never talked about me dying after it happened. No one ever talked about my hospital visit nor asked if I was ok. But during this visit, my mom just bluntly stated that while I was in the bed for two weeks that she saw, every day, a hooded black figure with a sickle watching me from the other side of the garden glass. She said each day he'd come closer until he was right up against the glass and then…he disappeared. That's when I woke up and regained consciousness at the end of those 2 weeks. I'd never told her about my angel of death experiences during asthma attacks.

=

Technically, coming back from death is a bit of a life hack, it's not a normal procedure, it's like a glitch in the system of the order of things. The body is meant to house one soul for the duration of that particular life story. Death is when the soul and the body part, so the soul can continue on with its growth. Most likely it will choose to come back to earth again, in a different body. The body decomposes without the energy of the Soul.

Returning to the same body it departed via death is due to the Soul's power to override what's taking place in the physical body. Only the Soul has this power, and when the human thinking mind is unconscious, the Soul has more room to make these kinds of powerful choices.

A common experience for those who come back to life, like myself, are the difficulties that occur afterwards. In my case, I found that many physical healing modalities will not work for my body, like chemical medicines but also many herbs and other natural remedies, and this even baffles the doctors and naturopaths. It's true that before this death and resurrection I had negative reactions to the many medications doctors gave me, but these intensified and expanded after and became poisonous.

Ever since my return, when I go to the doctor and they try to give me medicine, my body will not accept that: I will either have an allergic reaction, have no improvement from that medicine at all, or a slight and temporary change, or more damage, finding myself right back where I started before I spent that money and time. Likewise, if I invest time and money going to a naturopath/Chinese medicine/Ayurveda/functional nutritionist (and I have), taking the protocols that work for others, or even ones tailored to me, I have the same response, but they often cause eruptive inflammatory responses that don't resolve over time at all. Nothing can heal when it's in a constant state of inflammation. Chinese medicine has been especially brutal on my health, and other naturopaths give up. So what are my options? I've found that it's my Soul's desire for me to learn how to use my mind, to train its ability to create thoughts as medicine. And, to use energy to heal.

I could blame all the doctors of my youth who experimented on me and did harmful, illegal things to my immune system. I could be angry at them for causing so much damage and carelessly lying about the fact that what they did were known no-nos in the medical field. I could be upset at all the adults who were supposed to care for me who didn't listen to me at all and continued to make me suffer irreparable damage. I could also be angry that my family didn't help me sue the doctors so I could get money repair some of the damages...or I can believe that my Soul is on a path to discover its power to overcome physical limitations on its own despite what is thrown at it and despite what is thrown at the body it chose.

Humans tend to see death as a failure, but the Soul sees death as a door out of one experience and an entry into another one. A strong Soul may demand to stay in a body that offers it a specific timeline of growth opportunities even if death tries to interrupt that embodied experience. Having a strong Soul doesn't necessarily equate to an equally strong human, quite the opposite in fact, so that the human can grow through challenges and contrast, to learn what it is to become powerful in partnership with the Soul. Dying doesn't mean someone's Soul is not strong-the Soul knows what it wants, and that's what it gets.

Ever notice how people in hospitals often pass away while the family members have left their room just for a minute to use the bathroom or get a quick coffee or after they fall asleep for a quick nap? This happens when the Soul says "Enough! It's time for me to go!" and it takes that opportunity to depart the physical body when the relatives are not around, so it can depart free of guilt. The human thinking mind in that body will often try to stay long past what the Soul desires because of love for the family members still on earth, due to fears of dying, because of regret...there are many reasons why the human self and its Soul can be in different places, and this is the unique relationship we all have with our "selves".

As humans we tend to also see illness as a failure.

The reason a Soul comes into a body is because it wants to grow and know itself and so it chooses a very specific life path that's in opposition to what it wants. This is so the Soul can fully experience whatever it's looking to learn as an energy body (which is unlimited) fitted into a human body and thinking mind (which are very limited). So, the human limited self can learn what it feels like to overcome obstacles and grow in unlimited ways. The human perspective on life tends to be: I'm successful when I get what I want (money, love, career, fame, health, some endpoint that allows comfort), but the soul's perspective is: I can only grow when I take my human self into a challenge and come out the other side, like a snake shedding skin as its muscles grow and expand through experience.

If a Soul wants to experience unconditional love as a human, that Soul will choose to be born into a family that doesn't offer love at all, a family who may constantly try to gaslight the child and show the child they don't have value, and may even abuse the child. This serves as a challenge or opportunity for the human to search for love and its meaning, to trust its Soul push to move through these challenges and overcomes these limitations. If a Soul was born into a family that offered unconditional love, that Soul would have no desire to know what love is, because love is already part of its experience. And to "know" something, we first must be under the illusion that we are separate from it.

The Soul always knows what events will take place within the timeline it chooses. Souls don't incarnate in the same family line over and over-they are free to choose to incarnate in any timeline, any family any culture that the Soul finds a timeline within that will offer it the change to grow through adversity.

It's only a surprise to our human selves what unfolds in our lives. So, to merge the earthly consciousness (that is all about what it can see here as evidence on earth) and the Soul consciousness (that sees life through a much higher perspective and knowing) can be as simple and as profound as asking "what am I trying to learn from this?" when a challenge arises. From here, we can imagine our lives like an extended comic book or journey quest and map out what we are going through..to see what story is emerging from our Soul self.

The "hack" available to all of us, whether you've died and returned or not, is to practice living in both worlds, so that your very understandings of life and of death change. I think this is precisely what scares people most about talk of death and ghosts: the fact that the more you learn about this, the more your ideas about life might change dramatically. This seems to scare people more than talk about death. Because for most, death is something we may think about, but it's a concept, something that will occur at some point. But life, life is here now, and if our very idea of life is challenged, then maybe our very idea of ourselves might be challenged, and then, where is the truth? The truth might be held by no one and everyone, and it might be all about discovery. For some, discovery doesn't seem as solid as someone outside of yourself telling you what's right and wrong so you don't have to think about it. Humanity is concerned with acquisition: the soul is concerned with continually shedding the snake skin of smallness.

LOVE HEALS

In 1992 I moved down to Peck Slip in lower Manhattan, right on the water, a short time before I auditioned for my band Crisis. Peck Slip was a loft building owned by a talented and mysterious photographer who had a darkroom in his loft, plus two rooms for rent. At the time, this building's bottom floor was part of the South Street Seaport and sold fish during the day. I rented one room to live in, various artists rented the other as a workspace.

The owner had two black cats, brothers Aesop and Zephyr. Zephyr was antisocial and a hisser. Scraggly hair, scraggly claws, chubby and wild, he looked the way his temperament was, and he never warmed up to me. He didn't warm up to anyone really, but that was his charm. Aesop, on the other hand, became my dear friend. I was very allergic to animals when I first moved in, but Aesop was always around me, so eventually I began to wear a sock on my hand so I could pet him, because he always wanted to interact and be against my body, following me everywhere I went in the loft. He was gorgeous: long and sleek and slim, beautiful eyes, a perfectly handsome black cat. I really loved him.

I started working a soul-killing job in SoHo, and I'd come home after work and walk to the kitchen table, set my purse on the chair and just cry, heaving sobs. Aesop would come running from some corner of the loft, jump up onto the table, and begin to rub my eyes and cheeks with his forehead, effectively drying my tears. Somehow my allergies tolerated this. Then he began to spend time in my room every day. Id' always wanted a cat, and it was as though I had one now.

At a certain point I needed to move. I quit my job and had to find a cheaper place. I felt terrible leaving Aesop. We spent so much time together, I worried about not being able to communicate to him why I was leaving. In fact, the owner of the loft said Aesop cried in my room for a month after I moved out. Apparently he just stayed in my empty room day and night. I think a part of my heart never recovered from leaving him behind. After all, he had opened my heart.

I stayed in touch with the loft owner and a year or so after I moved out he contacted me to let me know he was going to have to put Aesop down because Aesop had stopped functioning. He had a seizure and could no longer walk and didn't want to be touched. So I was invited along with other friends to Aesop's goodbye party. I felt such a mix of emotions: guilt, urgency to see him and hold him, and a super sharp focus that told me I needed to see him and hold him and nothing was more important. I would let nothing get in the way of me seeing him. As an introvert who avoided social interaction as much as possible, this says a lot about me making the effort to attend a party with people.

I arrived and said hello to the loft owner, and while other people wanted to talk to me and catch up since it had been so long since I'd seen many of them, I excused myself went straight to Aesop who I'd missed so much. He was laying on a black fabric on a ledge looking feeble. I thought it was weird he was on the ledge, but the owner explained he didn't walk anymore.

I went to pick him up and the owner quickly warned me that he doesn't want to be touched but Aesop let me pick him up and I held him close to my heart, with his head on my shoulder, and we were cheek to cheek for 2 hours until I left. I didn't socialize with anyone, I just gave Aesop my apologies and lots of love, recounting in his ear all my favorite moments we spent together. I left that night, tears streaming down my face, devoting all my thoughts to Aesop.

The owner called me the next day and said Aesop was fine! He was now walking around! Due to these changes he was taken back to the vet and got a clear bill of health! In fact, the owner would move not long after that, and Aesop and Zephyr went to live at his friend's countryside farm upstate and they lived another 10 years of a great life, with full mobility.

That was the first time, but not last, that I'd learn I had a special connection with animals. Ever since that moment, black cats have always been in my life, finding me during intense times, and staying with me until the challenge was completed, whether for months or years. My own tuxedo cat Ernie taught me how to deal with ghosts and protected me during dreamtime as we took naps together involving astral travel. Then there were the strays and cats of friends, such as Vito, Moe, Vampiro, and 3 other black and white cats, all of whom would protect me during weird living situations within a span of 4 years, all with whom I developed a means of communication, or rather, we worked together on communicating, because they were all teachers too, they all were healers or allowed me to heal them.

And, whenever I'm working on an extended project that's about to reach a conclusion or that I'm having to continue in the face of challenges, my cat Ernie, who lived to be 21, sends me smiles and hearts from the Spirit world. The week before completion of a project I will see a sign from him every day. Sometimes I will put olive oil in the pan, turn around to see a giant circle with 2 eyes and a smile. Or I could be trimming paper edges, look down to scoop them up and see they are in the shape of a perfect heart. I could put some sodium bicarbonate in the sink to clean and it will take the shape of 2 eyes and a smile. I have photographed dozens of examples each year since his death.

OVER MY BODY

One of my most revisited childhood memories (a childhood full of illness and doctor visits) is of watching my mom and myself. My mom was holding my hand, comforting me while I lay in bed in pain and discomfort, wearing my favorite corduroy overalls. These overalls were dark indigo blue and had huge red, yellow and orange flowers on them. I loved those overalls and wanted to never outgrow them.

It was a sunny day, and as I watched us from ceiling height I enjoyed the wooden floor's warm sepia tones as some of the light shone through the window behind me to my left, causing a hazy golden glow across the floor.

My bed was against the wall on the right and I was watching my mom hold my left hand. I can see the top of my mom's head, and my eyes are closed, my face is tilted to the right a bit. The wallpaper on the left wall was white with giant orange and black flowers whose bold outlines I also loved to watch and explore with my mind on many days, a sort of daydream process I engaged with while asking big life and death questions. I was around 5 years old.

You'll notice that my memory is of watching the both of us from above. My memory is me out of my body while ill, watching my mother and myself. My memory isn't of *being* comforted.

I know that I'm in pain, as was common for me, but I don't remember how it feels. I don't remember the feeling of lying in that bed with my mom next to me, I don't remember getting into that bed. I remember watching us from above. That memory is burned into my mind. I've replayed it over and over again, and I can draw it in detail.

It wasn't until decades later, reading a book about someone else's Out Of Body experience that I realized this was one of my first OBE experiences, and that's what my memory was about. Reading the other person's story helped me understand why this memory, and others, were from a viewpoint that felt natural enough to me but also felt different. I just didn't realize why this memory was different until I real that story, which is why it can be so helpful to learn from others.

It's likely this memory remained so clear for me, and why I found myself revisiting it often, so that I could learn something significant about it at a time when I was ready to understand it in a bigger way.

I normally don't spend time in my memories: I have always been very forward-moving, and I only look back to learn and analyze briefly, I don't dwell. But the fact that it remained and replayed itself for me, because it had something important to teach me, is the beauty of how our lives teach us what we need to know from within our own personal experiences.

TRIPLICATE

In 2009 I received my Reiki Level 3 attunement, which is an initiation into the 3rd level or degree for using Reiki healing energy. Not long after this day, I found myself at home with a headache.

I rarely get headaches, and when I do they're noticeable. So, I decided to give myself Reiki to heal my headache. I made myself lie down on the right side of the bed which was on the floor. There was perhaps 6 feet of space between my head and the wall with loft windows behind me. The floors were wood, which I love. Wooden floors are my favorite surface and I feel a bit lost and ungrounded without them.

Lying on my back, I began giving myself Reiki, holding my hands on my head, drawing the Reiki symbols in my imagination and directing the flow of energy into my head. I thought to myself, "I don't really feel anything," when I suddenly found myself outside my own body, with my feet against the wall (or maybe even through the wall) with the loft windows, hovering maybe 5 inches over the floor, watching myself on the bed.

But I didn't just see myself in my bed. Next to the "me" on my bed was a transparent version of myself, also lying on my back but on the wooden floor with my left arm outstretched, touching my own head. In other words, I saw two of my selves healing myself, and I was watching this as a third version of myself behind those two, floating at the far wall.

I don't remember going back into my body, I just remember waking up feeling refreshed with no sign of a headache, and I remembered watching my selves, thinking that I should paint what I saw.

FLYING INDOORS

It was my first birthday party in public. I was 5. My mom invited my kindergarten classmates to McDonald's for a Ronald McDonald (the clown) theme party. Mc D's was a new thing in town and a big deal for casual dining.

I can remember thinking to myself, "I don't even really know these kids. I'm having a party with strangers. How uncomfortable." I didn't like being in a group of people, and I really didn't want to be there. The restaurant was dark brown walls and ugly toned tiles with deep red leather booth seats. I didn't understand why the lighting had to be so yellowed and horrible.

I became mesmerized by the birthday cake when it was brought out, which had a Ronald McDonald clown on it. I was really curious about clowns in general. On the cake he was holding a red and yellow balloon. I really really wanted to touch that red balloon decoration! So I did. And my eyelids began to swell and swell until they turned inside out. I was having a severe allergic reaction to the eggs in this decoration, so I had to be whisked away from my own party and taken to the hospital.

While in the hospital, I was walked down a long corridor of curtained rooms on either side and into a room at the end of this hallway where I was supposed to sit with my parents while waiting for the doctor. I don't remember seeing the doctor, I don't recall anything that happened in that makeshift room, but I do remember flying around the hospital into each of these rooms behind the triage-type curtains.

I'd been so curious about who was behind all these curtains, that somehow I'd left my body and was getting an up close view, floating into one room and then the next. They were all full of sick old people with tubes everywhere, sunken cheeks, some extremely thin old men, many machines. It was a horror show. From then on I hated going to the doctor and to hospitals, yet I'd have to return for many tests and medical experiments. I was not able to see these facilities as places that supported health. They were only full of pain and uncertainty. They were not places of hope.

NIGHT GATHERINGS

    I graduated high school early, and with the half-year remaining, I got a job at a local 99 cents store in Calumet City, the town where Buffalo Bill the killer lived in the movie "Silence Of The Lambs". I was also enrolled in two classes at a local college, which would then also allow me to apply those credits to my Parson's School of Art year, advancing me a bit more along that road. I seem to have a habit of often being ahead of the game in my life.

    The 99 cents store was in a typical American strip mall. There was a juice bar in the center of the mall square, and I occasionally got a juice or snack there. The 99 cents store itself was very small, one big rectangular room with some short shelving units running most of the length of the shop, and a square island of registers right inside the front door. The shelves were short enough to see over, even for me. There was a small office in the back that shared space with a table only big enough for one to eat lunch and the small employee bathroom.

    The first day I worked there I cut a vein in my thumb knuckle with a box cutter, as I saw in a premonition before it happened, and blood gushed upwards and outwards as if in a horror movie. Since I couldn't get it to stop bleeding even with pressure, my manager sent me to the emergency room for stitches.

    In a few days' time I was back at work, and I was working the night shift, which meant I'd remain there to clean up after the store had closed. On this eve, my manager was in the back room counting the register drawers, and I was alone in the store. I really liked it there. I'd never been one drawn to "things" as much as experiences, but I found it a delight to see striped socks next to pots and pans and all sorts of strange gadgets people had invented made of plastic, ceramic and fibers, all in bright colors. It was full of stuff both practical and silly.

    I finished all the other cleaning and straightening and was preparing to vacuum. The main lights were turned off, and there was a soft warm glow from the single light of the office in the back and some muted lights from the street shining into the front of the store. It was very dark in the room in fact, and I liked the contrast of the darkness with the soft glow. My duty at this point was to vacuum.

I was against the far right wall, bending over to plug in the vacuum when suddenly I felt my attention perk up, and my ears and back became prickly. Something told me to turn around.

As I, did I saw a very clearly defined but transparent man about 3 feet away from the far left wall, intently looking directly into my eyes. Though transparent, his image was quite detailed. The man looked to be from the 1920s based on his mustache style and clothing: dark blue almost black satin vest with a lighter blue print, a pocket watch and chain, white shirt with a stand up collar, thin bowtie, thick and curly mustache, dark short hair parted to the side, combed over and kept in place by some pomade. He reminded me of a barkeep. He was staring at me intently, and I just froze, and then I turned back towards the plug in the wall next to me for the vacuum and decided I was just imagining things.

Something told me to turn around again, and with some fear, I did and saw a woman had joined the man. She was on the left, he was on the right. She was dressed in a Victorian style dress with her hair partially pinned up, some dark brown curl ringlets hanging loose, with a corseted top, long sleeves and wide shaped skirt, holding her hands. Now they were both looking at me intently.

While it was common for me to sense ghosts and their personalities and even their images in houses of friends, relatives, and in my own home, I hadn't ever seen them take a solid form like this, and it threw me for a loop. It reminded me of cartoons with ghost characters I loved watching when I was little. The story lines were stupid, but I liked the idea of being invisible and flying around, defying gravity. Here I was with my own ghosts, and instead of investigating, I thought to myself, "I must just be tired and hallucinating."

This time I decided I would vacuum after all and forget all about this. So I turned on the vacuum and began to vacuum, when it got stuck. So I turned it off and looked behind me to find several dozen transparent people all watching me. There were adults, very young children, and ages in-between. They were now a crowd. It wasn't just that I could see them: I found feel them and I could sense the intensity in which they were watching me and their expectations. In my mind I thought "what do they want from me"!? I felt too much pressure from that question, and not knowing what to do I ran into the back with my manager and pretended the vacuum was broken and made a bunch of small talk with him. I think he could tell I was freaked out, so he compassionately let me linger there, chatting about meaningless things. Then we left the store together.

=

Because we are all built with more than one perceptive sense, we are all able to perceive other physical human beings as well as disembodied people in various ways beyond just what we see with our "naked eyes" and beyond what we feel with our hands.

It does not matter whether or not you believe in your Soul, it exists, and it is the energy-double of your human self. So, just as your physical body uses 5 physical senses, your Soul body also uses its psychic senses.

It does not matter whether or not you believe in your psychic senses, you're already using them: when you can tell your partner's emotions just by walking into the room, when you have a "gut" feeling about something, when you plan your dinner or an outfit to wear out in your mind. You're not using your physical senses to do these things, but rather your psychic senses of clairsentience (psychic feeling/sensing), clairvoyance (psychic sight), etc. Often your own preferences of colors or textures in clothing and furniture are based on your intuitive ways of connecting with the world around you even more than your physical ways of connecting to the world around you. Vibes, visualization, dreams, premonitions, and more, are ways of sensing beyond what is visible to the "naked eye," but we all use these senses on a daily basis, unaware a lot of the time.

It also takes time to understand how to navigate the psychic world of perception, to learn to discern clearly and not be deceived, to translate the subtle feelings, sensations and vision. Mostly because we are not taught about the universe from the perspective of the universe but rather by other humans and limited or stylized perceptions. And we are also taught to not trust ourselves, so it takes time to relearn how to do so.

For me, I was born able to perceive my physical world and also the invisible psychic world. I didn't have a chance to decide if one or the other was more real than the other, because my experiences with "seen and unseen" were equally palpable. Premonitions were a daily happening. It wasn't like my interactions with spirits were only in my dreams...they were part of my waking day, just as perceivable as my experiences of going to school, or talking to classmates, and perhaps even more real because I was using my other senses and I was able to perceive psychology, personality, truth and lies, all things that can be hidden in the physical human world, especially from children. Still, my learning process was one of unfoldment: it took time and practiced observation and organization.

Just because I could perceive in some ways didn't mean I knew what to do with those experiences. I wasn't aware of my options. It did mean that I had other ways of perceiving that needed development which I'd learn along the way. In my adult life I had 2 years of training under a teacher, which gave me a great command of my interactions with the psychic world and then also, by parallel nature, has given me more command of my physical world.

Spirits were very alive to me always, naturally. I never doubted their palpable presences even though I was the only one noticing them. And, while we transmitted information to each other, it was in a telepathic way where a collection of information was given and received without individuated words. It was always an inner "Knowing".

There had been many times where I'd walked in on a ghost conversation and could overhear the voices of the ghosts talking among themselves, but I'd not had a conversation like that with ghosts (in my earlier years) so I didn't even think to ask them questions, because I could just sense so much already. I was also aware of "ghosts" which I didn't like, and other "helpers" as I called them before I knew about "Guides in spirit".

These helpers were more difficult to perceive as a child: they didn't take the same forms as ghosts and they were more subtle, but they were always helpful, supportive, encouraging and respectful, so I had to make some effort to seek them and then receive their answers. Ghosts, on the other hand I noticed as a small child, were often grumpy or selfish or manipulative, invasive or sad...just like human beings.

That night in the store, I didn't think to just ask the ghosts what they wanted, and I also didn't think to tell them to leave me alone. Both were perfect options. Later I'd learn to communicate back and forth, to set appointments or refusals. I learned that, just like on earth, I can't trust someone to do what's best for me. I must establish those conditions and I have the free will and rights to do so.

At the same time, for ghosts who need help and for passed on relatives and friends who want to get messages to their embodied loved ones, spirit communication can be a beautiful, loving way to be of service and to learn about the potentials of human consciousness.

IRON LADY

Growing up I didn't really like my grandma. I had to see her every Sunday along with alpha male grandpa who was an angry, domineering man. She was unfriendly, very serious, and the older I became the more it seemed she disapproved of my goals and dreams and was trying everything in her power to prevent me from reaching them. I did admire how she seemed mentally impenetrable, however.

For example, when she would come to our house for dinner, she and my mother would go upstairs into my bedroom closet, take out all the fabrics and art supplies I'd bought with my own money I'd earned from selling my creations, and then throw them away. This started in my middle school years and continued until she and grandpa moved away to a retirement community in Florida. The Iron Lady was always sure to tell me I'd never succeed in having a variety of goals and interests.

No one in my family had a supportive word for me ever: not for academic achievements, not for violin and piano awards, not for sports achievements, not even for the scholarship I won to Parsons School of Design in New York City. I was beyond a straight A student, never got in trouble, and in my spare time I made things, sold them, and bought more supplies and repeated. Before I graduated high school I'd been selling my clothing designs at local boutiques and in Chicago, saving the money I earned, with ambitions to continue this while at art college.

One year things changed a bit, interestingly. I had to fly down to Florida to visit the Iron Lady. My mother, aunts and sister were already there. Grandpa had his 3rd heart attack, and having already survived a triple bypass, he died within days. The Iron Lady got to be with him in his hospital room before he passed, but she had developed a c diff bacterial infection due to the hospital over-medicating her. This hospital cared for retired people and over-medicated them often. Carelessness was common. So grandma couldn't keep food in her body, because the medication killed off her good and bad bacteria, and they thought she might also die. I arrived for the funeral and to possibly say goodbye to grandma as well.

By the time I got there to visit, she was back at her home, but the Iron Lady had gone really soft. She could barely sit up, her head was drooping over, and she told me she loved me, which made me think she knew she was dying because she was not usually affectionate.

During this visit I found a small health food section at the local grocery store and was happy to find their free magazine. I didn't have a computer, but health food stores were becoming more common, and I had started to study some natural healing methods for myself through these free magazines and the remedy reference books these stores tended to have at their locations. I'd healed myself of some issues this way, so I knew from experience that new possibilities for reclaiming health outside of doctor offices were available.

In this particular magazine I saw an advertisement for a probiotic called Acidophilus. While probiotics are common these days, the 1990s, it was a new thing in America.

Not long after flying home, I had a dream about the Iron Lady. She was shrinking and becoming teeny tiny, disappearing. My mom, sister and I made a circle around her with our arms linked and she began to grow back up to her full size. I awoke and called my mother, asking her to move my grandma away from those doctors and into her own house, and to also give her acidophilus. My mom did, after the time it took to pack and sell the house, she moved the Iron Lady in with her and her new doctor gave her acidophilus and she would live another 10 plus years, until she was just a year shy of 100.

Some time passed, and after grandma was settled in my mom's house for a while she suddenly developed another c diff bacterial infection. I received the call late at night from my mother - she said the doctors didn't think grandma would make it through the night and they wanted her to prepare. They said they hadn't seen a c diff so bad and it wasn't responding to any treatment after days of being in the hospital.

I had recently received my 3rd level of Reiki healing training, within 7 days from this incident. So I decided, once I got off the phone, to send as much Reiki as a I could to grandma. I sent energy for about 45 minutes, but oddly, I didn't really see much or feel much. During the previous levels of Reiki training and healing work I'd done, I usually saw vivid colors and patterns of energy going into the body, and I could also see tumors or illness in the body and the organs. This time I felt and saw almost nothing.

So, I went to bed. In the morning got a call from my other that the Iron Lady was fine, and nurses and doctors had no idea what happened. They apologized for not being able to explain it. She never again got c diff.

The next couple of times I'd visit her during the next decade she was much kinder and even told me that she would have made similar choices as I have in my life, but that was frowned upon in her time (being an independent woman). She told me she did love grandpa, but she was happier without him. She became much friendlier to me on subsequent visits, and transferred her coldness to my sister.

A decade later when she was 99 and her pacemaker was not working well and she'd lost hearing and sight enough to sadden her (she was a social lady with her church friends and she loved to read books), I knew it was her time. My mom invited me to come say goodbye but told me not to show up with any of my crystals and do anything to grandma. While I had never told my mom I used them, I could tell she wanted to have her own magic moment with her mother. I couldn't in fact come, thought I felt my grandma waiting for me.

So the Iron Lady peacefully passed away with my mom at her side at home with hospice care, and with a "ding" from the grandfather clock in the room (that grandpa made but had stopped working).

The way I'd find out the Iron Lady had died was on a day when I had to take the J train to downtown SF for work. At this time, I had a morning meditation practice after which I'd observe my jars of dried herbs that my Italian mother-in-law shipped me from Italy, along with tree barks, walnut shells, sewing needles, and more treasures. I'd then pay attention to which ones offered themselves to me. I'd take a pinch of each herb, wrap it in a small paper, and wear it in my bra for the day. I only looked at the names of the herbs *after* choosing them. And, I might also do some research about them through my work day to find out what they were offering me, but mostly I let the natural objects guide me throughout the day.

On this particular morning I rededicated myself to this historical reclamation my Guides-in-spirit were teaching me regarding Italy. After, I took the jar that called to me and wrapped some of the herb: White Willow. Then I realized I was about to miss my train and I ran out of the house to catch it. As I hopped on the train I realized I'd forgotten my phone, and I instantly heard in my head "people are going to need to reach you today", but it was either stay on the train or be an hour late to work.

I stayed on the train and opened up my notebook and decided to work on a song for the upcoming debut album of my band Gospel Of The Witches. I didn't have any melodies nor words written yet for this song, but as I turned on my ipod and opened my notebook a flow of lyrics poured out and I wrote them down as they came, which was not my usual process at all. The chorus was "I reclaim..." I could hear all the melodies in my head, and while I didn't have my phone with me to record the melodies, I knew I'd remember them.

While at work I snuck in some research on the computer and learned that White Willow supports reclamation! Then, an hour before the store was closing, the manager told me I had a call form my mother and sent it to my phone. I didn't know my mother even knew where I worked. Apparently she'd been trying to call me all day - the Iron Lady died in the morning during the exact time I was on the train writing those lyrics.

=

It would be months till I'd go visit my mom after the Iron Lady's death. It was after all the daughters picked over grandma's things and after mom did a little rearranging of the house. During those months grandma did not come visit me in spirit. It made sense, we didn't really have any unfinished business.

During this time in my life dragonflies would find me on my walks, or they'd hover near my eye line as I'd look out the window. This magic creature would find me everywhere and remind me of magic in everyday moments.

The first night I spent at mom's house, the Iron Lady awoke me and let me know she was doing just fine in the spirit world. She told me to go look inside her jewelry box which, unbeknownst to me at the time, was on my mom's dresser on the far side of the wall. I located it, opened it up, and found a singular object waiting for me: a little metal pillbox the diameter of a quarter with a jeweled dragonfly on top.

"WHITE WILLOW"

I RECLAIM...
the ancient ways for which I've burned
for which I hid
from which I ran...
my ancient guides call me from the hearth and its flames

I RECLAIM...
to dance under the moon again
and in the sun too I shall rise, in phoenix light

I RECLAIM...
I hold my path blessed again,
blessed again

through my heart all the treasures are
handed to me
glistening upon the golden bough she gifted to me

Dear Mother, Dear Guide,
blessed is this Light
blessed is this Light
blessed is this Light
Blessed is this Light

copyright Karyn Crisis' Gospel Of The Witches, 2015 from the album "Salem's Wounds"

SEEING THE FUTURE

It's possible to see the future in a variety of ways: seeing many possible futures at once, seeing the future in terms of coming concepts/societal shifts/group changes in consciousness without knowing exactly how they will play out on an individual level, and seeing the literal future: 15 minutes from now, an hour from now, etc.

The way I'd seen the future since childhood was mostly in terms of: possible futures and potentials, and then experiencing them playing out, such as reaching my goals, being in danger and who was going to harm me, political happenings, group dynamics, and also dreaming of people I would meet; AND outcomes such as yes/no, societal shifts and small changes indicating much bigger life changes for groups and individuals conceptually.

During my time of training at Spiritualism school, and in my personal training time with my Guides-in-spirit, I was learning about different rates of vibration: different speeds of frequency and what types of knowledge and conscious beings could be acquired and met there. For me, I noticed that Guides felt very fast, high, and bright in terms of frequencies, and that I'd get to feel their super fast energy within my own body mind and spirit, along with a feeling of expansiveness and light.

I noticed in contrast that slowing down my vibration and relaxing deeply, would help me connect with passed-on earthly people. While the initial meeting with any spirit was best made on a high frequency (because that allowed me to hold a high quality meeting space), continuing the communication was best served in a slowed-down way so I could see the memories they were sharing with me, etc. This would lead to me seeing the literal future.

Towards the end of 2014 I was invited to be part of a psychic fair at an organization in a different area of San Francisco. I was interested and agreed, knowing that it would be a totally different crowd of people attending: younger and more culturally contemporary, and also I knew it would be a potentially messy group of psychics: some self-made, some trained, some who used drugs, etc. Ultimately, however, I felt it would be a good learning experience to give my style of readings to people who I'd likely not meet through my school.

I had been focusing, at school, on giving Mediumship readings and intuitive readings for a group of people I didn't know. At the start, however, I'd sit quietly ay the back of the room and try to "prepare" by taking an energetic look at the group to see if there were any spirit people hovering near embodied people, so I'd know where to start when I was in front of the group.

Due to my own desire to grow and as prompted by my Guides-in-spirit, this time lessened: perhaps I'd arrive too late to prepare, or other things would take my attention, so I had to learn to jump into readings with absolutely no prep time. Considering this, I decide to push it a bit further for the psychic fair. I would sit with my back to the room so I wouldn't be ale to see the other people, nor would I see who was approaching me for a reading. I had a little bowl of water that I'd use to break connection and reconnect in between clients, more as a reminder than anything else.

The way it worked for the fair is we would sit in our chosen areas, awaiting clients who would choose readings from us based on our biographies and sign up sheets from the tables in the entry way. Organizers for the fair would direct clients to their reader among the 3 different rooms we were seated in.

Before this even started, I chose to shut out everything by closing my eyes and meditating, finding my own space within the ambient noises, connecting with my Guides-in-spirit, dipping my fingertips in and out of the water occasionally, allowing myself to slow down and be in the present moment. As I did, I felt a female person approaching me from the main room, slowly reaching out their arm towards my shoulder, and very gently touching me to attempt to let me know the festivities were about to begin. I thought, "Hmm, this is a funny thing to see in my meditation!" and then, perhaps 2 or 3 minutes later, this exact thing would happen physically, I'd feel that gentle touch on my shoulder, and I'd turn around to meet the female coordinator who was telling me people were being let in now.

In between each session, I would allow myself to relax again, dipping my fingers in the water. I was surprised to see a very clear image (in my imagination) of an animal from a deck of oracle cards a friend had gifted me. I had only used this deck for myself, choosing one card each morning and reading about the animal and its spiritual attributes, as a way of encouraging myself to feel connected to learning lessons for the day. During this psychic fair, however, each animal's lesson was exactly related to the person who'd sit on the chair across from me to get a reading. The cards were showing me the answers to the queries each person would be asking about when they say in the chair.

GHOSTED

I grew up in a haunted house where a group of ghosts lived, and most of my relatives lived in haunted houses too. If we took care of a friend's dog in our house, they would bark at the same areas of the house where I felt scared to go.

My grandmother often recounted family ghost stories at meal gatherings. The one I remember most is of her as a child, wearing her brand new church dress. Her family was Depression era poor, so a new dress was a big deal. After church this day, her cousins invited her down to the lake to swim. She knew she should go back to the house and change into her swimsuit, but then she'd miss this opportunity to get down to the lake with her cousins. They were going now. So she chose the lake and had to swim in her new dress and had such a wonderful time.

When she snuck back into the house, she became very sad, knowing she would get in a tremendous amount of trouble for ruining her dress. She was so stressed about it that she started to feel sick, and put herself to bed, in her wet dress and all. Later, she woke up to her mother's concerned face, checking her forehead to see if the fever had gone away. But my grandma was not wearing her dress. Her mother hadn't taken it off, no one had. My grandma insisted she went to bed wearing it, so the whole family hunted through the entire house looking for it, but it was never found, even after days of searching.

Years later, when they would move out of that house, everything was being packed up into boxes, and the movers decided to check the attic. Grandma's mother tried to dissuade them-she said they didn't have a ladder to reach it and hadn't had one for years. The movers used their ladder, went up, and found Grandma's childhood dress from the day at the lake, neatly folded and in perfect condition.

=

The town I grew up in had a well-known, rather infamous haunted house on one of its main roads that connected 2 other towns. The house had a semi-circular driveway owned by my relatives (I never met them). It was a weirdly dark brown house, and it almost created its own pocket of darkness on an otherwise busy, business-filled street. The house was infamous because it couldn't find a permanent buyer. My relatives would try to sell it, someone would show interest and the "for sale" sign would come down, and then due to the ghosts the new buyer would abandon the house, and the "for sale" sign would go up. Over and over this cycle went, and apparently everyone in town was aware of this story, which had legend-type status, long before I heard it.

=

My eldest aunt had a large house on an even larger plot of land near a river. Every time we drove there I got excited to see the horses that live on the land next to theirs, their giant backyards full of trees, hammock and walnuts from the trees. The backyard was so large it felt like being on a campground, with free space to wander and be alone with my thoughts. At the same time, I felt a certain amount of dread every time we drove there knowing I'd have to feel the creepy, grumpy ghosts in her house.

This big house, even though it looked fresh with white walls and lots of windows, jazz music playing on speakers throughout the house and some modern fashion magazines for me to look through, had 2 really grumpy ghosts who didn't like me at all and they definitely let me know it.

Bathrooms have always been my safe space away from ghosts, whether in my own house growing up, houses of relatives, at hotels. Only once did a ghost enter the bathroom, but he also left when I demanded it. In order to get to these safe spaces, as a child, it usually meant I'd run there, feeling the ghosts chase after me.

My aunt would love to tell the story of her son claiming an "angel" would put his blanket on him sometimes at night as he was falling asleep, but I knew it no angel-I could see the the grumpy, territorial lady who really disliked me, as she told the story. I was already aware of this lady from my previous visits to my aunt's house, and I knew this grumpy lady also had a grumpy husband, and both these ghosts followed me around this house.

One winter day I wore my brand new purple jacket. It was quilted and had a huge hood. I really hated most clothing styles of my generation, but I loved this jacket because on the cold winter drives I could just sink inside of it and fall asleep and lucidly dream. I really disliked being cold, and it seemed I had to be in the car often, cold, in the winters-waiting for my mom to get out of church, or these hour and half drives to my aunt's house. This jacket felt like a magical solution. Just sinking inside of it I felt protected.

I'd only had it for a couple of weeks when I wore it to my aunt's house. It was particularly grumpy day for the ghosts. The relatives put my jacket in hall-way closet. After a super long time there, during which the ghosts had given me no space at all, it finally it was time to go. There was no jacket. We searched the entire house, no jacket. I had to take the long drive home coat-less in the middle of midwestern winter. My mom later phoned all the relatives to see if anyone knew anything of the jacket, but the it was never found.

OCEAN OMPHALOS

One of the most profound experiences I've ever had was in Manasquan, New Jersey. In the very early 1990s, my boyfriend invited me take a weekend trip to his aunt's house which was on the edge of a man-made lake that was in the center of town. Houses were built around it, and many of them had boats docked which they could use to go visit their neighbors or move around town. It was a strange sight, arriving at night in a town built around a lake. It was also very dreamy, like something out of a fairy tale.

During this time of my life, post-Parsons School of Design and still living in Manhattan, I was rather depressed. Ever since I was a child, I'd been trying to find a place that felt like home; some place to call my own that had a small lamp which I could sit under at night time, alone with a book, allowing the atmosphere on those pages to come alive and dissolve me. I thought art school would be home, but it wasn't. I didn't fit in there either. So I didn't re-enroll for the next year. Disgruntled teachers, old thinking, rich kids with no passion: it was not the art school I wanted, there was so little life and exuberance there. An art student classmate of mine was awarded the highest grade for our sculpture assignment: he made a Marlboro cigarette box.

My sculpture was a towering inferno of fire made out of cardboard and metal scraps, and inside the fire I had a boombox playing industrial noise music I had recorded that was supposed to be the sound of sorrow and despair in my heart. My next project was a Nancy Grossman inspired high-backed wooden chair. I built it from scratch and covered it in black faux- leather. It featured heavy buckled straps across the chair back, and the seat was a bed of nails. To give my sketchbook more atmosphere, which we had to fill with boring color wheels, I dragged it through the streets, gathering dust and puddle water, crinkling the pages and wearing down their edges. One assignment that offered some freedom was a map-making project. The only rules were that we had to include a guide showing the 4 directions. My map was the head and torso of a body, whose inner world showed the map of the loss of its soul.

I was there on scholarship. I thought they'd fail me, because I was always pushing their thinking, pushing my teachers to examine their own complacency, burning like a fire. I was at odds with everyone there, one of my classmates said "I'm here because my daddy wants me to." They offered me another scholarship, but I turned it down.

In the meantime, I'd moved into an apartment of artists, but I didn't fit in there either. I realized, after moving in, that the couple in one of the bedrooms were heroin addicts as an ambulance came to resuscitate the boyfriend who overdosed. I was just not finding any place that felt like home.

So this particular weekend my boyfriend invited me out to NJ, I thought it would be great to take a trip on the train somewhere new. We arrived at night time, ate a snack, and left our things in his aunt's house. After talking to his friends on the phone, he took me on a short walk out to the ocean. It was probably midnight. In the blackness and quiet of the night, some of his friends met us there, and they began to chat as I examined the beach. It was a shallow shoreline of sand, and there was a very long jetty of large, scraggly rocks that went out into the water. That's where I was drawn to.

I left the group to their talking, and made my way to the rock jetty. The wind had picked up to a howling roar, and I pushed against it to move forward. The rocks were much taller up close, more difficult to climb than I expected, and they were much more jagged, with lots of water splashing around between each rock. I thought to myself that I could easily fall into the water and be lost. The waves were quite intense, jumping into the air. It would be difficult for anyone to try to pull me out of this treacherous space if I fell in. But I was being drawn out to the end of the jetty, and I finally made my way out the the last jagged rock and just stood there, feeling the wind whipping against my cheeks.

I noticed how dark the sky was, how clear the stars, how lovely the black ocean water looked under the starlight, and how, even with the strong wind, it was so silent. Then it became even more silent. The water lost its waves. I began to lose sight of the horizon line. I could no longer make out where the sky ended and the waterline began. The stars disappeared, the water was still, I was no longer standing on rocks. I was weightless; I could sense no above and no below, I could sense no "me", but I could feel everything, everyone, and everyplace, and it was this sense of "feeling" rather than the sense of "knowing" that made this experience so very alive. A doorway of perception had opened, and I was experiencing something beyond what I knew to be life in this sometimes disappointing earthly world. I realized I was in solid blackness, like the void, in complete stillness and peace. I was feeling bliss, embraced by space, by something I trusted to hold me up in what felt like a cloud of nothingness. I felt connected.

I suddenly heard a loud sound breaking through the absolute silence, a male voice next to my ear that said "HOME." I realized, yes, this feels like home, this beautiful, velvet soft blackness. The voice also startled me, being so loud and disembodied, and I became aware of where I was again as the rocks came into sight and I panicked a little about about how to get back to the sand. The rocks seemed much further apart on my return than when I first climbed out.

I would remain haunted by the experience, having felt at "home" at last, and then having it slip away as I came back to the daily reality that: I didn't feel at home anywhere. My artwork began to obsess over the word "home" and my search began again, which at first just took me much deeper into depression. I realized some basic nuggets of truth then, even thought I didn't know what to do about them: no one, no place, no thing would fill me up and give me peace. I knew that only I could give myself what I needed, but I didn't know how to do that quite yet. I knew that I felt so alone because other people couldn't see me as clearly as I could see them, they didn't understand me the way I could understand them without even having us say any words. I longed to be held by that peace again and I searched for it over and over, not finding it anywhere, until many years later.

=

Something happens with spiritual awakening.

First, awakening is a process and you will awaken again and again.

Second, it can cause a deep grief and sadness as you gain this enormous perspective about eternal life. You realize that the people you meet are part of your life story, and you find it precious, even the painful parts. You realize you'll never get everything accomplished that you desire. You realize the pain you will feel when your lover is no longer in physical form-and by then you'll realize you'll be able to feel each other as energy, but something about this terrible, clumsy flesh you will miss.

Third, you will realize that everyone is on a path of growth-which means that even if you think you found your ideal lover, your "forever" might not be forever if you are growing in different directions, but that it's necessary for you both to have the freedom your Souls need in order to grow.

Fourth, you may be fortunate enough to recognize not one, but dozens of people who come into your life as having shared a life path with you before.

Fifth, you may also feel like you're a secret invisible person on a movie set that is only occasionally noticed: you are the helper, the observer, on the sidelines, and at the same time you feel a deep deep love for the people around you, no matter how messy or unaware they might be. You realize how short life is as you remember your past lives, and you realize how soon it will be that you're onto your next life.

Sixth, your own preferences about things in life dissolve-material objects don't matter anymore, and the things that open your heart are the things that can't speak your same language, and in ironic contrast, you realize that you can communicate with: plants, light, water, animals.

Seventh, you realize that some of the weirdest things about being in a human body are the things that make you most feel alive. And, you start to realize you've not been in the wrong place at the wrong time at all: you belong everywhere you find yourself.

FIRE IN THE NIGHT

One winter in the mid 1996 ish my band Crisis did two tours with the same 2 bands. We were moving through much of the midwest I think, maybe south east (it's not easy to remember locations for me, after visiting one club after another while driving for a month in a van) when things got a little intense.

On this particular afternoon, we 3 bands all arrived at the club and set up our merchandise tables and began to survey the stage and unload gear and do all the behind-the-scenes work that has to take place before the evening show. The other 2 bands were more famous than my band and we were the opening act.

A particular young blonde lady was following me around, and she made me feel uncomfortable. The doors hadn't even opened, this was supposed to be time for set-up. But, being in a band, I was having to learn to be social with all types of people, so I did my best. She was a groupie-type, having come early to meet the band members and get some attention. She spent too much time giving me compliments for them to be sincere and I could see through her tactics-I knew she wanted something. At a certain point, she suddenly leaned in and told me, "I'm going to watch every move you make and copy you and get more famous than you are," with what I guess was supposed to be her threatening stare.

I was used to this behavior. Many people were fascinated with me because I was maybe the second female to front a creative metal band and tour nationally (and then also internationally) extensively. I was a rarity. Also, my vocals were a combination of feminine melodies and heavy growled vocals, and it was a surprise to people that a woman could make those sounds. I was very short and elf-like, and offstage I was very kind and warm-in contrast to all the power I embodied in a very masculine way onstage. So often, there were guys trying to bully me at the merch table, or other young women pretending to befriend me so they could get in favor with the guys in my band. People regularly wanted to test me. These types of people were dime-a-dozen at shows and I could see them coming from a mile away. I was great at reading people and their intentions before they even said a word.

I made my way to the bathroom to get some space from blondie, because she kept talking at me about herself and I had work to do. In the bathroom, often my sacred space on tour, I could breathe and feel free of that. And I received an unexpected intuition: I realized I needed to introduce her to the blonde singer of one of the bands. He was a funny and sweet guy, a regular dude who was always looking for flattery from pretty females, and she just wanted attention, and I felt I was clearly supposed to introduce them. After all, I realized, it might get her off my back and give myself some space. I was a little worried she'd take advantage of him because she was aggressive, but it felt like something I was *supposed* to do outside my own selfishness. So I did, and sure enough, within minutes they were inseparable and having a great time. I was a matchmaking queen, and I also didn't have to deal with her focusing on me anymore.

It would take me many years to learn that it was *my* responsibility to set boundaries with people and to teach them what was ok and not for me. I mistakenly thought that being nice to people would create a pleasant atmosphere, but instead it often led to people taking advantage of me. People who are manipulative can sense the quiet types who just want everything to be ok, and I had to learn to not trust people to do the right thing for me: it was *my* responsibility to protect myself, *my* responsibility to speak up for myself. It is not someone else's responsibility to do the right thing for me.

In the morning, after driving through a really long and messy night after the show full of intense snowfall and poor visibility, we arrived at the next club to an eventually strange scene: all the band members of the other 2 bands (who were traveling in the same RV) were late to show up and when they did, they were all wearing identical clothing that wasn't really their style: shiny dark bomber jackets flannel shirts, and brand new stiff pants and boots.

Apparently, during the long drive, one of the tires popped on their RV and started a fire in the gas tank while the guys were sleeping in their bunk beds, and it quickly spread through the van, destroying money and personal property and stranding the guys on the side of the road for a time while much of the RV melted away. They lost everything that was not in the trailer.

The fire started in the blonde singer's bunk, and he would've burned or even died considering the fire started as an explosion, except for the fact that he was not in his bunk. The girl I introduced him to invited him to stay with her that night. He did, and she drove them to the next show in her car.

=

Another thing that happened through me frequently on tour was: saying just the right words and the right time to someone else that helped prevent an accident or otherwise harmful issue.

On this same tour stretch, pre-show at the Stone Pony in New Jersey, we band members were all doing the usual pre-show set-up of: merchandise tables, unloading gear from the trailer and rearranging it onstage, checking out the back-stage area, trying to eat, writing out guest lists and set lists, etc.

I was walking from the stage area towards backstage area through another small room when I saw the blonde singer of the band again. We'd become easy pals, always sharing a good laugh about something or another. I didn't spend much time backstage on this tour because it was full of guys drinking and acting tough and lots of female groupies baring it all to get some attention and it was all too sleazy for me, so I moved around like lightning when I needed to get something from backstage, keeping oriented at the merch table.

This particular night, I had to walk back and forth a few times within maybe a 15 minute period, past the blonde singer a few times. He was sitting on the edge of a circular brick pedestal that had a fire in its center, like an elevated indoor fire pit. There was a black rounded grill over the fire, and it may have even been electrical, but it was really warm, even hot. The 3rd time I walked past the singer sitting there, I said something like "be careful you don't melt your pretty hair in that fire" because, well, his blonde hair was long (its was almost the entire length of his back), he was proud of it, and he felt it attracted women to him. He was very attached to his looks.

I moved quickly into the backstage room to grab a water bottle when he came running in after me in a panic and showed me that he had indeed singed all the ends of his hair on that "fireplace." He was freaking out "Oh my god, oh my god, my hair! What will the ladies think! My hair! The chicks love my hair!" He was horrified.

Fortunately I had given him that warning when I did, though it was really was just a funny thought that came through my head at the time, because the fire had melted about an inch and-a-half of his hair all across the bottoms, and a little more in some places. If he'd have stayed there longer, who knows how much damage would have occurred. He begged me to give him a haircut trim right there and then, which I did, reassuring him that the chicks would still find him hot.

=

Sometimes I just had the right words to jolt someone out of a depressive place, or the right words to encourage someone with their dreams. Sometimes I also channeled exactly the right fighting words: being one of the few women to ever tour across the U.S, at that time, bouncers and security guards tried to give me a hard time often, or deny me entry to my own sound checks, so quick words that chopped their manhood down to size in a rough way they understood were my key to shocking them back to some decency. This was not my normal way of talking. I learned that people remember my words, positive and negative, long after I had spoken them and forgotten them.

=

I learned so much about myself on tour. My psychic senses helped me survive. I often knew things before they happened (if a show would be sold out, if a promoter would rip us off, if there would be violence at a show), I could tell who was trustworthy or who was lying, and I discovered I was a healer, though I wasn't ready for it at this time.

I noticed people began telling me with more frequency as each year passed, that my voice, lyrics or the music as a whole helped them through their darkest years, helped them overcome addiction, and more. People seemed to need to hug me after shows, and after shows I was always glowing. I called it "catharsis," because I too was transformed with each performance.

My intention with singing was to open my heart and just let all the rawness out. No pretense, no trying, just very real, raw, humble, vulnerable. Due to this, my performances were something I called "summoning" I felt it was me "plus extra energy" that I was channeling. And I often said I felt the band was us members "plus extra". There was definitely a presence overlooking the band, and when the members got selfish, that presence brought things to a halt. Looking back on my lyrics, there are many spiritual ideas in there that you will recognize from ancient spiritual traditions, spoken my way.

I was called a shaman before I knew what that meant. Onstage I was flying out of my body for sure, and I felt plugged into electric socket and full of superhuman power, and this power cleansed me, made me more than my limited human self. With this energy I could do anything. I was very aware my daily life Karyn was something less. This power was not just for me: it either healed, empowered or uplifted those who liked it, and it pushed people away who were fake, insincere and not ready to be self-aware, like the old male guard who wanted women only look a certain way and who were absolutely threatened by my presence.

I felt my music was a duty, and my duty was to "serve the work" as I called it. The 1st show I ever played was at CBGBs in the lower east side of Manhattan. I didn't really enjoy it because it was full of other peoples' opinions about how my mic stands should be, and since I followed other peoples' opinions I wasn't able to feel free and unleash.

The 2nd show I ever played, at a small little place in the lower east side, a ridiculous club called Brownies where the "sound guy" (I use quotations because this guy was a hack) was chasing us around with a db meter saying the drums were too loud!

I wasn't really looking forward to this show, but a local musician named Marc Sloan spent some time talking with me. I confided in him that I felt nervous and didn't really want to be onstage in public. He gave me advice that would change everything. He said something like "Karyn, sing for the people who have no voice." That changed my whole perspective, and from that night onward I kept those words in my heart and that's when the channeling, the summoning, began.

ANGELS IN THE DARKNESS

When my band Crisis made albums, there was a procedure we followed: we'd write the musical part of the songs in rehearsal. I'd draw, make notes and comment on arrangements but I would write my vocals and full lyrics away from rehearsal, when I was by myself. We'd rehearse the songs well, and sometimes we'd test out the new songs during live shows before recording, preferring to break them in and settle into the energy, to really have them feeling like a part of us. That way we were more prepared for the challenges of studio recording. Over the years, I'd occasionally feel confident enough to leave small bits of my vocal melody placement to be worked out in studio, but mostly I liked to be prepared. We never had much time in studio and I wanted to get the best out of myself.

The writing for our album "The Hollowing" was very different because we were going to stay in Metairie, Louisiana for a month and record the album there. Due to the production schedule with our label, I had to make the artwork beforehand, even though I was still writing lyrics and working on melodies. And, this artwork was quite ambitious: I'd built a marionette puppet with a hinged door covering over his heart, with a sculpted removable heart inside. I also built him a coffin out of balsam wood, painted with wood grain and inlaid with hand-quilted green silk, and drew a set of city buildings on large card stock.

I photographed all of these scenes with the idea of showing a man in the throes of despair, with a hollowed out heart, preparing to send himself and his hollow heart out to sea in a coffin. So I had to photograph these scenes, keeping room for lyrics and credits which would be inlaid later. I also printed the photos myself on fiber paper, sepia tinted them, and vignetted the edges in black all with my Duerst photo enlarger and chemicals in my makeshift photo lab. It was quite time consuming (pre-protools, using a manual camera-Minolta srT 202), and as a result I didn't have time to complete my lyrics and vocal melodies before taking our road trip to New Orleans. I was stressed out.

I'm not a musician-I can't jam and create. I don't do well in-the-moment of that live creation that my band was all about when writing songs. I had a process where I'd go into altered state with just my mind to find the story the song was trying to tell me. Sometimes that meant I'd reach for a word while listening to the band, and become fascinated with that one word I'd hear emerging from the atmosphere of the guitars. Then I'd trace the historical trail of this word through a very old thesaurus which offered optional words choices with similar meaning, along with interesting facts or historical anecdotes about words. Sometimes I'd free-write and put the writings together later, when I wasn't listening to the music. Simply, I'd be taken on a journey and a story would be revealed to me if I could listen and watch well enough. It was an extremely anxious process for me, but now I realize I was trying to get myself into a trance state so I could channel the songs.

In fact, the songs were not really written *by* me: they were already written and would show *me* how to sing *them*, all I had to do was listen. I didn't have much choice *but* to listen and sometimes try to place new notes in the right positions according to the personality of the song. I was never able to jam like many musicians...I needed to listen to the air to hear the song teaching me its parts. Often the notes were out of my vocal range, but I was able to "stretch" my voice into those new places. My role really was to write the story with words, the simplest words possible that expressed the most. I felt this was an inherited rule and duty given to me: express maximum meaning with minimum words and melodies.

During this album process in general, throughout 1996, I was feeling very, very sad and low and I was finding it difficult to turn these sensations into something creative.

The first 2 songs I recorded were the ones I'd already written, which were "Mechanical Man" and "Fires of Sorrow". "Fires of Sorrow" was a song I'd written about my dad's death, a sort of send-off. When we'd perform it live onstage I felt the desire to wear wings, so I made a large set of wings with a balsa wood frame, flexible armature wire, and flex foam feathers that I cut out and stitched onto the wires. I didn't realize it at the time that this was a very psychopomp effort, one that would become a part of my life as a trained Medium.

The control room of the recording studio was downstairs. There was no windowed recording room attached to it, as is often common. In this traditional set-up, the producer and or engineer are in the control room, and they can view the band in the next room through a window (small or large). The entire band, or one member at a time, is set up in that other room with microphones or direct-boxes so their sound can be recorded without any ambient interruptions. It's like a giant isolation room.

This studio didn't have one of those rooms, so I chose to set up my vocal recording mic and headphones in the tiny upstairs room, which was in the corner of a larger open room. I would have to communicate with the producer via microphone and headphones only. This was a good thing, since some of the songs were very emotional for me to record, like "Fires of Sorrow."

But then I had to move along to write the other songs while the guys were continuing to record their guitars and bass downstairs. We had recorded the drums in Brooklyn, New York prior to coming down to Louisiana.

So I continued to work on my lyrics and song development in this little room. It had only one door, like an office door with glass slit, no other windows in the room. The only lights were 2 bulbs under green light gels.

This room opened to a larger room (directly to the front) and sort of hallway to the right. On either end of the hallway were doors leading to: a balcony on the far end, and a staircase going downstairs on the near end. There were NO white lights anywhere in this room or hallway, only red, blue, green lights. This time, like others, those lights were turned off. It was quiet and I was alone.

I was painfully trudging through the album, and slowly completing many many of the songs but I decided to focus on "Surviving the Siren" and I was very stuck. My mind was burning with frustration and I was tired of pushing. It was so unnatural. Sitting with the tape deck, rewinding and rewinding, re-listening...I just couldn't get past the first stanza *"On beaches of bones, the sirens sing, and you cover your ears, but it's the song you used to sing..there's no escaping as you are pulled into the sea."*

At a certain point I was just so sad, tears streaming down my face, feeling so very lost. I was close to giving up but I hadn't and I hadn't given in and instead started asking for some help and then screaming (inside myself) for some help to make some forward movement. Suddenly there was an immense light that filled the doorway area: it was bright white, almost hot and blinding. I looked up, and even though in its enormity it felt like a giant floodlight, my mind tried to make some rational sense out of it and so I then thought maybe someone opened the door and the light from the other room was flooding in.

The light moved towards me, and I demanded "Who's there?" almost angry to have been interrupted in my personal hell (and forgetting that *I* was the one who asked for help after all). The light became even larger, like a huge aura, and it came close enough to almost blend with me. I was filled with a great peace, a sense of love, the complete opposite of what I'd felt before. I was just in the light. I have no idea how long it lasted. I just know that after that all the words flowed and the song was completed.

After completing the song I was so excited and I ran downstairs to ask the guys if someone had come up and they all looked at me strangely. Of course they wouldn't barge in on me, they all said. I explained that a bright white light blinded me for a brief time. The producer reassured me there were no white lights upstairs, and he even came upstairs with me and turned on all the light switches. There were only red, blue and green, and they didn't make much light at all, it was very dark, even in my mini room.

=

Later that day I'd have 2 more experiences with white light. Downstairs there was a hallway whose lights were burned out. The bathroom, whose door was on the left side of the hallway, also had its lightbulbs burned out. The studio owner was notified but hadn't come into studio yet with bulbs, and there were no more left at the studio. The only other lights were the ones inside the studio room, whose door was left open to allow some ambient light in the rest of the studio.

While there were no working bulbs, I was walking down the hallway while thinking of another song I needed to complete and suddenly there was a blinding bright light above my head. The next time, I was sitting on the couch outside the studio, and I was alone in the darkened space that opened to the hallway. There was just a little ambient light. I was also thinking about completing songs here when the room in front of me filled with bright light. My mind tried to make rational sense of it, so I assumed it was the guys returning from the store with some bulbs and yelled out "hey guys" from the couch, but no one answered, and then the light faded away, and I was left again in the dark.

All my songs were completed that night.

WISDOM OF MY VIOLIN

When I was very young, 4 years old, I started writing music. I called it my "siren song" because it was torture: I loved listening to music, but when I tried to make music, I would hear songs in my head yet could never make them sound the same way on an instrument outside of my mind. I was passionately obsessed with music and yet it tortured me by only letting me get so close.

During my early single digit years of childhood, I had a mini organ/keyboard type electric thing. It was tan and it had 4 tall legs, which was perfect for my miniature self. My dad's acoustic guitars and harmonicas were usually laying around so I played those, then eventually in my middle school years I'd buy a Korg poly 6 synthesizer and a Gibson copy guitar from a thrift shop, borrow my friend's bass and record my music on a 4 track. I had the electric blue Boss digital delay pedal and loved to play with the effects, adding a microphone to my collection.

In my in-between grade school years I played piano and became obsessed with violin. I made my own out of a cigar box from school with a wooden paint mixer stick and rubber bands, making sure to use different thicknesses so I could make different sounds. I was determined, by 2nd grade, to go back to eastern Europe and be a violin-playing gypsy like my great grandfather from Transylvania. Eventually my mom got me a violin and I became 1st chair 1st violin in the school orchestra, and eventually in the youth symphony orchestra of Chicago I was 1st chair 2nd violins among people much older than I was.

In middle school, there was a super cool guy who took my bus. We both had 80s hair being that it was indeed the mid-80s: buzzed short on the side and swept over curls that came to a long point in the front. Sometimes we would chat about British dark pop and synth music and experimental music. I found out he lived only one street over and that his mom was a private violin teacher, teaching out of their home. They were Russian and had escaped there to come live here.

His mom was gorgeous: tall, thin, super long dark wavy hair, huge eyes, she was always cooking octopus and slathering her face with vitamin e oil, and her skin had no wrinkles. She became my teacher and took the makeshift tape frets off my violin: in school the teacher cut thin clear tape and taped it to our violin necks so we could find the notes. She told me I needed to hear the notes before I placed my fingers down. She also supported my love of darker, mournful violin music.

And this started another tradition of mine: walking home after school on the side roads by myself instead of taking the bus so I could listen to the silence. I'd talk to my violin in my inner thoughts and it would teach me how to sing, offering me melodies and teaching me to hear the notes before I sang them, but even more so to *feel* the notes in my throat before I sang out loud. Sometimes I would sing the notes the violin was giving to me on those walks, paying attention to how my throat would feel while as I did, paying attention to how small adjustments in my lips could change the volume of my singing.

Ultimately I learned from my violin how to *feel* my voice and how to know what the *feelings* in my throat meant, and I learned how to *hear* the notes I was meant to sing before I made any sounds. I learned to *listen* to the Universe and my own body, and this ability to listen has been integral to my creativity. From listening to my violin, my throat and voice, and to the Universe, I learned:

+diaphragm breathing
+belly breathing
+how I was able to know if my whole range was working or not with a simple test
+what foods might help if my throat was out of balance
+how to rarely lose my voice, and what it meant if I did
+the impact of allergies on the throat, sinuses and more

I later found out these are things that have been taught by other people- I learned them from the Universe. I also learned I couldn't use the remedies other people used to keep their throats in shape, such as the steamer. Using a steamer dried out my throat and affected my lungs when I tried it. It doesn't matter if famous people have used it successfully, my body rejects it.

A few famous singers in other metal bands started emailing me for advice. Some of them pretended to be singing coaches after that, based on what I shared with them, not giving me any credit of course. Whatever it is I desire to learn, I simply have to ask and then *listen*. This abundance also calmed my anger and hurt when people would steal my lyrics or other ideas, because I it showed me I never have a shortage of ideas when I listen.

I would use this idea later to do what I called "stretching" my voice to reach ranges that I wasn't previously able to reach. I didn't have any training as a singer, my idea for training myself was simply to do was practice singing some notes out of range and imagine my voice was stretching to reach them. And it always worked.

When I joined my first band, in which I used a lot of guttural sounds and screaming, I never lost my voice, unless I got the flu, due to my ability to feel my voice in my throat and listen to its guidance. If I got the flu, my lungs would fill with fluid and I'd be coughing non-stop and this would definitely cause me to lose my voice for days. But generally I could sing for 30 days in a row and not lose any of my range nor vocal power.

=

After I left my first band, I didn't sing for a few years. Then I was invited to sing on en Ep for Italy's Ephel Duath, then a full length album. Not long after that I'd record the debut album for my next band, Gospel Of The Witches.

In each case, I sang out loud for 2-3 months prior to recording, and that was it for the entire year preceding each album. The vocals I recorded were quite challenging range-wise, but because I channel, that power and ability to reach those notes just appeared. While I had to put in a lot of work, daily singing, my ability to channel helped me acquire entire new ranges of vocal notes, without any training at all.

=

Everyone can learn to listen to their body, body parts, inner organs and emotions. It might take a little practice, but if you can consider that any issue like a symptom or emotional reaction is a messenger trying to get your attention, you can approach issues with a curiosity or like a reunion with an old friend.

Or, you can talk to whatever you feel an affinity towards: trees, animals, the ocean, clouds in the sky...when you're really seeking an answer, and you focus intently on your question, and demand an answer come forth clearly, it's possible that answer may come as you push. It may come seemingly directly from the cloud (if it frees you up enough from your own mind) or it might come later when your mind is occupied while you're sipping coffee or doing something in a relaxed state when your guard is down.

For some people, physical activity brings mental clarity, and when the human thinking mind is relaxed, the intuitive mind of your Soul can receive answers from the Universe, as it's meant to, because there is no resistance. For some people, creative action is the key. To others, its might be trying some unfamiliar territory, such as connecting with nature if you don't normally try to do so.

Receiving messages, just like speaking with an old friend, requires give and take, asking questions and being receptive to responses.

I HEARD IT FROM THE TREES

I found myself teaching the advanced Mediumship class for a Spiritualist center after our teacher, a certified Medium, left the state. Before he left he'd been preparing me for more responsibility. But after he left, it took focus on my part: there were not so many people who trained under him who knew the protocols so I often found myself alone making important decisions.

I was on the Secretary of the Board as well, and it was my job to protect the bylaws. But as a teacher, there were no class materials to draw from. I had trained under him for 2 years, quickly advancing, and I was also taking the Morris Pratt training for certification, and I felt the Spiritualist spirit guides helping me, quite clearly. I took this job seriously and wanted to do my best at helping the students expand.

During this time I was also running each morning at 5 am in the forest, through the trails, and I found a little hill, often guarded by 2 ravens and peppered with pine cones, where I'd rest when I was done, before going to work. Each evening I'd run to the ocean.

I noticed I felt very comfortable at a certain spot and it was between 2 trees on the hill. So, I began talking with the trees, telling them my concerns, my questions and queries, and then...when I stopped talking so much, I notice they were talking back to me! So I visited them often, and they started giving me lesson plans and exercises.

Later, a student at our center went to the Arthur Findlay College in England. I wanted to attend but it was very expensive. When he returned, he told me that the lessons I was teaching them were the same techniques taught at this expensive college. The trees gave them to me for free. In fact, he apologized for resisting some of my instruction. He took it more seriously from this expensive school, but acknowledged that he was assisted in the exact same way by me first.

=

One of the things Spiritualism teaches in the historical Morris Pratt classes is that Spiritualism, and the ability to be a channel, is an equal-opportunity ability. There were many stories about poor people, women, people of color who had tremendous disadvantages in daily life, and yet, with the help of Spirit, they were able to cure themselves back from the brink of death, deliver inspiring speeches, make geological and astrological discoveries, write important works of philosophy, and more, even in the presence of skepticism, deep cultural criticism, racism and sexism.

I'd later learn this through experiences as well: that any knowledge can be reclaimed because the Spirit world of helpers is alive, they have access to all knowledge. If you are meant to learn some of that knowledge, you can learn to work with helpful Spirits to receive it, and then in turn, help others on the planet.

In this way, knowledge is free, whereas many societal groups and even spiritual groups create hierarchies that you have to pay into or be voted as worthy of by other humans. There are many human-made obstacles, but energy, and knowledge *is* energy, is not limited to human obstacles. Seek with your heart and doors can open!

The key to working with this "eternal, infinite encyclopedia" as I call it, and its keepers, is knowing that you can't do it all alone. Ego won't open the door. Connection, love, devotion, aspiration, expansion, trust and even vulnerability will. In this way also, this knowledge is protected by its keepers. It can't be forcibly taken.

It is possible, however, to take some knowledge in a sort of ego-state, forcibly as in against-the Laws of Energy. It can only be taken with the assistance of dark spirits, in the absence of Light, who also trap the human users into being used as well, a sort of 2-way vampirism. When people are using knowledge that seems of a "magical" nature and it's being used to control others, it never contains Light.

Light and Dark are not the same thing as Light and absence of Light. Light and Dark are an infinite loop, one that ends and begins, begins and ends. Light and absence of Light, however, refer to Polarity. The Universe is based on Polarity, some say. And in Polarity, there is Light (Source, all that is in alignment with the Laws of Energy, if which Free Will is a part), and the absence of this. Because Free Will is a Law, souls can choose to work against the Free Will of others, but since this is against the Laws, they must get their energy from somewhere other than Source, such as human beings and their souls. So it's not possible to work with dark spirits who are part of the absence of Light without those dark spirits also feeding from you as well as feeding on others *through* you.

Polarity itself is a force that works to keep balance. That balance maintains equality-but that equality exists in degrees. For example, if there is an extreme positive belief in someone on the planet, someone else must have an equally extreme negative belief in order to create the balance. It's like twins of the opposite, but not just of people, also of beliefs, thoughts, emotions and the ideas they create.

THE SAVING GRACE OF DISEMBODIED VOICES

During my grade school years, I would regularly be taken out of school to visit doctors at Northwestern University's medical facilities in Chicago, Illinois. They performed experiments on me similar to experiments I endured was I was 6 years old. Here, they would scrape skin raw on my back and then drop liquid allergens into the wound and record the reactions (how much swelling, how red did it get). Then they would give me little toys. After that, they would inject other liquids shallowly under my skin and wait until I started having an asthma attack or swelling or throat-closing and then they would give me more injections to calm down the reactions. I was a human lab rat. It was very sci-fi.

One of the doctors there, a famous one, started making me take prednisone shots and pills when I was in second grade. I knew something was wrong with this approach-the medicine made me feel terrible and I wasn't improving either, but the doctor and nurses wouldn't listen to me. One day a Voice told me the pills were poison and encouraged me to stop taking them. I did since I agreed, and I felt so much better! My mental clarity returned, my skin cleared up and my body felt less jittery and anxious.

During the next visit however, the doctor figured out I'd been secretly not taking the medicine, and instead of accepting what I had told him before about how bad the medicine made me feel, including how it affected my mind, his answer was to sneak my mother out of the room (she was resisting more injections too) and he instructed a nurse to force another injection into me without telling my mother, while I was alone in the room.

That same Voice would help me understand what was going on in my body, and it reassured me it would help me when I was older and free to move away. We would do some repairs then, it told me. Meanwhile doctors kept pumping me with so much steroids I got moon face syndrome and other complications. The voice gave me the courage to stand up for myself (I was extremely introverted) and fight against these doctors that were severely overmedicating me. These days, the poisonous consequences of topical steroids and internal cortisone are well known among people with eczema who are trying to survive the great pains it causes. It was also known in the days I was a child, but it didn't stop doctors from experimenting on me, all the while normalizing deception year after year.

This Voice would help me in between my middle school and high school years when other doctors and their student doctors decided I should put steroid ointment on my body, then a thicker cream on top, and wrap my limbs with strips of fabric, like a mummy, and sleep like this every night. In the mornings I'd have to take the non-sharp edge of a butter knife to scrape all this off and then shower.

The Voice helped me notice little lines on my skin, where to me it looked like my skin was thinning out. The doctors gaslighted me, saying I was just getting fat, and they insisted I continue. They wanted me to do this for an entire year inside a hospital, which meant I'd miss my chance to get out of my town and go away to art college. I absolutely refused. In fact, the stretch marks got so pronounced that the doctors and student doctors stopped seeing me, refused to see us actually, because they realized they had disfigured me. When I told another dermatologist this story years later, he said I could have sued them, because every doctor in the industry knows it's a known danger to wrap skin with steroid cream on it precisely because it will dissolve the skin, and so it was never ever done. So fortunately the voice helped me stand up for myself since authority, yet again, did not.

In 1998, my band had just finished up a national tour and retuned to New York City. I had some rough eczema troubles on that tour, and I tried to take some herbal remedies to help but they increased the pain and skin rawness. A bandmate found a Chinese national doctor in Queens, and I took a long train ride to meet this man. His office was in an apartment high rise, and while he didn't speak much English, I recognized his setup: acupuncture and natural remedies.

He was very kind, and I loved the acupuncture. I often almost fell asleep on the table. He was giving me small brown lunch sack full of: bark chips, bug exoskeletons, plant pieces and herb slices. I was to boil a specific amount in a specific amount of water and cook it down to a thick consistency (basically, a small shot glass of liquid), and drink this. Daily.

It was brutal- this drink kept pulling out toxins through my skin, so I was raw and in a great deal of pain. While some detoxing is beneficial and curative even, prolonged detoxing is simply inflammation, and the body can't heal in a state of inflammation. He had big plans for me to see him for an entire year, graduating soon to snake blood. But at this point of spending my last money from tour and several months time of being in pain, I had to give up.

My band had a 2 day show at CGBG's coming up in just a few days that we put together. We had invited bands from several cities as far-reaching as New Orleans. I was so embarrassed because it was the middle of hot summer, and I couldn't exactly wear long sleeves and pants onstage to hide my skin. Our shows were really physically active, and I was so distressed about having to show up looking like a science fiction creature, not to mention these herbs made me feel like my skin was on fire...so sweating on stage in this condition was really tough to imagine. My entire body was covered with hot, painful, raw broken skin.

Then came a day when I was walking home from the train, after what I decided was my last appointment. This treatment was too painful, too expensive, and I was in tears. My skin felt like it had thousands of small cuts and someone was squeezing lemon juice in them, it was an active, sharp and hot pain.

I was about to walk past the local GNC store: at this time period, GNC had a small natural foods and remedies section. I occasionally went there to just browse and learn. It was only one small section of 4 shelves. I was also too poor at this time to really afford anything. But, as I was walking, in despair, I heard a voice, masculine and quite commanding, saying "look at the Tea Tree oil" and then I saw an impression of a little white jar of cream with green lettering. I had no idea what Tea Tree oil was. I had never heard of it and I didn't know what to do with it.

Entering the GNC shop, I went to the small section and there was a little white jar of Tea Tree Oil ointment. It was $13.00, but at that time that was the equivalent of $200 for me. So I went home empty-handed. That night, unable to sleep, I heard the voice again. The next day I went and bought that jar of cream. I put it all over my skin and by the very next morning my entire body had somehow calmed down, and by the day after (one day before my band's shows), my body was completely healed without a single trace of burning, red, cracked skin.

=

There would be other times helpful voices would call my name, encouraging me during challenging periods. I heard them out loud in the room near my right ear, usually upon waking in the morning before the challenge would begin. Or, I'd wake, in that early sleep state, in the midst of a gentle lucid dream in which I was being comforted by someone, feeling truly safe and loved. This was always a sign that something very scary would happen that day but that I'd be protected and make it through ok.

And then, occasionally there would be voices that weren't welcome. Such as one winter when I came home from school, knowing my family would arrive much later. When I unlocked the door and opened it, there were voices inside arguing loudly, so I remained outside in the snow until they arrived hours later. I had been looking forward to staying inside alone, with a hot green tea and my journal, eager to do some writing.

Other than that, the voices I heard were helpful, encouraging and factual.

TIME JUMP

While on tour in my band Crisis somewhere 2004-2005 ish, we were driving a long haul from one city to another during rush hour. We had a 15 passenger van and large trailer with all the gear in it, a heavy load of equipment. Driving with a trailer is always tricky, because there's a lot of movement from the trailer which only has two wheels and is attached by a hitch with wire connections for brake lights, so extra caution needs to be taken for the weight and instability.

We were also full aware of the more recent accidents that bands had been experiencing due to icy roads, long drives, and traffic jams. In fact, there was a band we knew whose singer had his legs crushed when their van crashed into a truck in front of them.

I had developed a habit, many years prior to this (1993) where I'd ask the 4 angels I perceived to stay on the 4 corners of our van. At the time, I didn't know anything about the 4 directions nor the specific Archangels. I was just aware of angel presences and for some reason I always felt secure asking each of them to protect a wheel and its corresponding van roof corner, especially because I was often traveling in the back of smaller cargo vans, lying on top of the guitar cabinets during our hours-long drives to play shows. Things were no different during this drive.

Traffic began to get thick and heavy, but it was still moving right along. The road was a bit unusual because there were no shoulders to pull off onto, but rather just a steep embankment with a gravel edge that dipped down into a grassy field.

I was in the bench seat directly behind the shotgun seat watching the road ahead between that seat and the driver's seat in front of me to my left. Suddenly, the traffic ahead of us began to come to a screeching halt in all the lanes. At first it seemed far away from us, many cars down the road, but quickly we noticed all the lanes to the right of were screeching, swerving and smoking from seizing brakes. We felt alarmed watching it all happening, that feeling of being more awake than ever, trying to urgently find a solution.

Our driver/guitarist began to slam on the breaks, knowing that we could not turn off onto the steep embankment to our left: our trailer would alligator-roll, and our van as well, and likely we'd all be severely injured if not killed, and the vehicle and trailer (which we did not own) would be destroyed. At the same time, I was worried that our driver's legs might be smashed as he tried to avoid plowing into the van in front of us and I was trying to change the vision of that in my mind.

Even more smoke was coming from tires of vehicles all around us slamming their breaks, our brakes were smoking and screaming, and the van was just not stopping nor slowing much. It was a symphony of urgency. There simply was not enough time for cars to find a way to slow down safely or even drive off the 5 lane freeway, no time to lose the momentum of fast speeds. There wasn't room for us to change lanes, because the road was packed with cars. It was such a weird scenario, like being in several future options at the same time but not being able to choose any of them, like when you feel yourself slip on ice and you have that slow-motion moment of being suspended in the air and suddenly you're super aware that you should do something but you can't prevent the fact that you will fall.

I screamed in my mind to the angels for help, and suddenly the van in front of us took a sharp and immediate turn down the embankment (and was fine), giving us some more "legroom" for our smoking brakes to somehow take hold.

After sliding down the road for what seemed an endless amount of slowed down time, I saw that our van stopped inches from the truck in front of us, and I leaned back against the back of the first bench seat behind the driver and passenger seats and said "it's ok, we're ok, we're ok, we're ok," and took a deep breath back into my body.

However, my bandmate in the shotgun seat turned around and looked at me with a strange expression. He asked me how I knew. "Knew what?", I asked. He asked how I knew we'd be ok before the van even stopped. I was confused, I told him I saw that we were ok, what was he talking about?

Apparently, I'd seen the positive ending to our almost-accident and sat back in my seat saying "we're ok" before the van actually stopped and danger was averted. I lived the present moment before it occurred for everyone else.

DATING IN THE TWILIGHT ZONE

Several days after I saw all those ghosts in the 99¢ store, sometime in 1991, I was at the juice bar during my work break. A guy I'd seen there several times with long hair and tattoos asked me out on a date. He seemed older than I was, probably by several years, and since I felt older than all my peers, it felt comfortable to me.

I was about to move to NYC in 2 weeks to go to art college. So the timing was a little weird, but I chose to go with the flow. This guy picked me up in his vintage car and took me to a small bar/restaurant that was typical looking for the midwest: small rectangular building with low roof, made of ugly grey bricks that were neither dark nor light, more of the color of "old", and a small neon sign. From the outside it was the type of place you'd expect to find lots of old grumpy men inside who wanted to drink away their domestic lives.

The inside, however, reminded me of a David Lynch movie. The ceiling was white, bright and sparkly white, the floor was carpeted in a deep but vibrant red. There was mood lighting, so the colors were very red with neon purple here and there and some warm white. A jazz band was playing against the right long wall, and because the ceiling was so low, they were super loud. The bar counter top was was a swerved snake shape, made of white and sparkling formica that glistened under the mood lighting and wiggled from the front door to where the jazz band was, halfway through the room.

People were very friendly. I noticed it was mostly men. As we moved slowly from one end of the bar counter to the other (near the restaurant seats), a few men in satin jackets with thin black lapels, very 1950s, kept saying hello to me, and a few bumped into me, and I had several very brief conversations. I thought it was a little weird that no one asked for my Id, but I didn't know the rules and had never been to a bar before.

My date looked at me strangely during dinner. We were seated in a red leather booth, sitting across from each other. I don't remember what I ate, but I remember quite a few people walking past the table saying "hello" to me. I remember thinking how strangely crowded this small place was. After all, it just looked like a dive bar outside, but inside it was full of people moving around, and many of them were wearing those fancy jackets. I was so interested in the surroundings that I didn't realize until later than my date wasn't really talking to me.

After we ate dinner, he drove me home in his car in silence and before letting me out, he looked at me and said "Ok, I just need to know what kind of drugs you're on." I was a total nerd: never drank a drop, never tried a cigarette, definitely hadn't tried drugs. I had a personal belief that I needed to face my pain, so I didn't have any vices other than art and music. I was so embarrassed and asked him what he meant. He said I was talking to thin air all night, and that I was having conversation with people who weren't there.

=

Palpable psychic phenomena like this are not uncommon for children, for people who are working on opening their psychic abilities, and for people who are natural Mediums (meaning they "find" themselves suddenly having these experiences), all without taking any substances. These phenomena are actually occurring by effort of the spirits who are making contact: whether earthly ghosts or Guides in spirit. The spirits are doing all the work here, and their purpose is to give us an experience that's hard to deny, in attempt to inspire us to question what took place and to seek answers in the world of spirit. It's a form of encouragement.

There have been many times in my life where helpful spirits (Guides) communicated to me through another person or manifested themselves solidly enough to give me a delightful moment, to offer some guidance, to point me in a direction literally, to protect me, and encourage me. While the majority of my communications with spirits and Guides offer me impressions, I've met many people in spirit who presented themselves palpably as earthly embodied people at the start, then something occurs to indicate no one else saw this person but me, similar to my date night experience.

Just as spirits can appear looking physically solid to whom they choose to see them, spirits can also move physical matter, make things appear suddenly (like placing a feather inside a closed box), and transfer physical objects from one place to another. At the same time, not all spirits have this capability. For someone to move physical matter while living fully in the non-physical world, they must know how to do this. It's not automatic.

Levitation is not a talent some human beings have: it's a phenomenon where spirit people lift and move a human being. This can be done by spirits who understand how to change cellular matter, and so these types of spirits are the ones who can create Transfiguration and the controversial ectoplasm. Healer spirits, referred to as Doctor/Healers in the Spiritualist general category of guides are ones who can create instant healing based on their ability to change cellular structure.

And then, there are more advanced possibilities: for human beings to be able to do things far beyond what seems possible while embodied in physical matter.

ENTRANCED

In 2016 I flew to Italy by myself for a personal quest. I didn't really have a plan, just a desire inspired by a visionary experience and a focus on visiting one place. I ended up traveling northwest, northeast, center, and south, thanks to invitations from Italians who invited me on journeys they seemed to know I needed and who introduced me to people who seemed to be waiting for me.

The original idea I had was to go to the region of Campania to meet with an author named Carlo Napolitano and his friend Jenny Capozzi, to visit a specific area called **lo Stretto di Barba**, where there is a river in a strange area between 2 mountains, a legendary place where the walnut tree of Benevento allegedly stood. Historically this tree was a place where witches would gather at night and fly off into the astral realm to learn secrets of the universe. And, it's a place where the Goddess, according to legend, physically manifested herself on earth.

Around this river, spread out a car ride's worth between each one, were 3 one-room churches that are considered to be protective charges by the locals, having been built on top of much older pagan structures and whose odd placements create a triangle, the kind of triangle associated with the Great Goddess. By protective charges they mean structures that mark sacred places which are guarded by spirits who protect them by either: scaring people away by creating psychic phenomena or inviting people to the place and giving them information in the form of memories or secret knowledge.

I learned about all of this because my husband had visited Benevento maybe a year before I would go by myself, while we were completing our band Gospel Of The Witches' debut album "Salem's Wounds." He brought back Napolitano's book "Il triangolo stregato. il mistero del noce di Benevento" from Italy and gifted it to me. Then, he verbally translated the book for me while I transcribed it into my computer, all while being pulled into visionary experiences and trances while doing so.

What I experienced while transcribing was being part of a circle of women who were dancing around a fire and generating energy that was for healing. The energy made a very specific pattern and was in colors that I recognized being part of other healing modalities (that is not a part of common knowledge). My trances seemed to be induced by the passage in Carlo's book that contained an invocation allegedly used by women to astral travel to the tree of Benevento.

So my reason to journey to Italy was to meet Carlo, visit this place, which would require me to visit Ceppaloni, Avellino and Benevento, and find out the truth about witches from interacting with local people.

I'd find more than I could ever imagine, learned more than I can ever share. And, it all started back in the California before I even left for Italy, when I would say that invocation in Italian every morning and every night in my meditations. It acted like a honing beacon that connected me not only to that place but to the secret knowledge and it source, and it connected me to all the resources, people, places and things I'd need on that trip. I'd even begin to find walnut shells at my feet in California when thinking about Italy, so many that I started to collect them.

I would meet up with Carlo, and he would take me to **lo Stretto di Barba**, and it would be wild. I would meet Jenny and I would return for the next few years too. But perhaps my journey on the way there would be just as amazing: for example, not having a plan and yet, just 5 hours after deplaning in Genoa I was walking up a mountain almost 3000 feet in the air to meet the last *strega* healer of the area in Triora, who I was told was waiting for me.

Then, after my adventures in the Ligurian region, I was to take the train and meet an acquaintance in Rome.The only issue was my phone wasn't working as it was supposed to, and I was unable to text my friend. So I decided to enjoy the ride on this *Frecciarossa* (fast train) and drink in the beautiful sights from my window. I was also people watching, and I noticed a guy who looked like a fan of metal and hardcore as I walked to the bathroom, and then later he walked by me too, as our eyes met.

As the train was coming into Roma Termini station, and despite the free wifi, I wasn't able to call nor text my friend to find out where we'd meet. I didn't know what else to do but follow the crowd. This crowd and my train car were near the back end of the train, so this crowd went down some steps, not knowing I could have exited towards the front, and that exit would've taken me to the main part of the train station where my friend was. Instead, I was at the back near rental cars and still couldn't get my cell phone to work.

I tried asking the police in my limited Italian, and they told me 9 blocks away was a wifi cafe. Nope. I didn't speak enough Italian to make any other conversation, my translator didn't work without wifi, so I just decided to go outside and enjoy the fact that I was in Italy! After all, there was nothing else I could do. It was sunny, there was chaos of Rome, people and cars and noise everywhere, so I just started walking against the train station, smiling, and even laughing and how happy I was, just surrendering to the present moment. I suddenly saw the metahead guy, who smiled at me, and I remembered how to ask him to use his phone in limited Italian. He let me, I was able to connect with my friend, and a quick hug to the nice guy and I was on my way.

I found my friend, and despite the rain he took me to Diana's temple which was on private land surrounded by public land. My friend found the owner and we were able to go in! Then, at Sutri we got there just in time before they closed...and at another spot, the Etruscan forest was closed, but we snuck in anyway and took photos. There I discovered a prayer habit I received from my guides in Spirit was also done here: writing down requests and wishes and burying them under a tree.

After other adventures, I boarded the next train, which was to take me on on a long ride down to Benevento, arriving at almost midnight. Trains here are not like trains in NYC or the Bay Area where they come often, and if you miss one you can just take the next. In Italy, you need a ticket with a seat number (on non-local trains anyway) for a specific time. If you miss it, you have to buy another ticket and try again if there's another one that day if at all, and sometimes the only other train of the day is sold out. Also, you have to wait in a room for the train tracks to be announced...and often they are usually announced only 5 minutes before departure, at which time you have to rush through the station, through crowds of people, and down the track until you find the exact train car you are supposed to be on and the exact seat number, all with luggage. For me, it was stressful, but I told the train station that we were going to be friends somehow.

So I got on the train, relieved that I managed that, and along came a group of people to sit exactly where I was sitting. This car had 2 seats facing 2 seats. I showed the man my ticket in case I had the wrong place, and he found we had the same ticket, so he gave me the seat. But then we realized mine was for next week. I'd mixed up the date/day. He spoke just a little English (most people in Italy don't), and told me to just stay in the train car and take an empty seat and I could pay the train ticket agent a fee and continue on my way. Considering my phone didn't work and the man discovered this was the last train of the day to Benevento, I hoped it would work out!

I took a seat, but, people kept rightfully taking my seats with their tickets, so I'd have to move again, and then again, and then there was only one seat left on the entire train car...right next to the guy who had my almost same ticket whom I met at start of all this mess. So he helped me when the ticket agent came, and I was informed of the cost I'd have to pay in exact amount to stay on the train. I opened my wallet and had exactly that amount of euros and cents and not a cent more! I bought my seat and settled in.

When I eventually met up with Carlo, he had both a day plan and a night plan for me with this area. First was the day plan, and he drove me to each of the strange churches, but I wasn't content to just drive by and stop briefly at each of them. So I asked him, well I told him, to leave me at the first one for an hour or 2 (at the most important one), so I could try to make my way down to the river where the witches were rumored to have gathered. He agreed, although he was very worried for me, because that area is also patrolled by the military, since people are drawn to it due to the legends.

After he left me there on the tiny narrow road, I crossed the wall and crawled down to the railroad tracks. There was just the wall (for the road), the railroad tracks, and then to the right was very thick, dense foliage, and I could hear the sound of the river. I tried to see how far down it would be to climb, but at this zone, there was just a sheer rock cliff down to the water, it was not doable here.

So, I decided to walk in a certain direction on the tracks, again, just so happy to be here. I pulled out my video camera and noticed there was a walnut shell at my feet. As I kept walking, there were more, as if they were leading me on a trail, one by one. But try as I might, I couldn't find a way into the wall of foliage and down to the river that wasn't only dangerous getting down, but near impossible to imagine getting back up.

I kept walking, being pulled by the walnut shells, and came to an overpass where the ground gave way and I was able to look down on the river from these tracks clear of the land and wall. I could see a very small patch of sand and some big rocks in the water and a piece of garbage. Since someone else had obviously gotten down there, I told myself, I will be able also! So I kept walking following the trail of walnut shells that was now increasing in number with each pile. Suddenly there was a pile of at least a dozen walnut shells at my feet. As I bent over to collect them and put them in my plastic bag, I turned my head to the right and saw, low to the ground, a tiny little opening at the base of the bushes and trees. I walked over and had to get on my belly and slide my way inside, forgetting that it was viper and scorpion season.

Inside, I saw among the dense low lying bushes and trees, a faint earthen path winding down. I would still have to crawl down on my belly like slithering serpent, grasping onto tree roots and earth to keep me from falling, but it was doable and I would be able to climb back out. So I did, zipping my hair inside my vinyl motorcycle jacket, twisting and turning, carefully sliding down this overgrown path until..I finally reached the river and the tiny patch of sand!!! And there, on that 24 inch by 36 inch patch of sand, was a singular walnut shell.

I sat on the large stone on the river's edge after I gave my offering to the greenery on the riverbank. I listened to the river singing to me, then I returned the favor, and back and forth we sang in the afternoon sun. I texted Carlo (my phone worked down here, in all odd places to work) and asked him for another hour's worth of time, and he generously agreed, for the crazy American.

That night, which happened to be a full moon, he would take me down to the church again and leave me there alone (at my request) even though he was panicking about doing so. You can read about what happened there in my first book "Italy's Witches and Medicine Women Vol 1". After, he took me for an incredible Neapolitan style pizza in Ceppaloni, really the ONLY kind of pizza worth eating.

=

Everything that the Universe decided I needed on this trip was gathered, rather magically. Italian people were waiting to give me interviews that answered all my prepared questions as if they had received a list of them ahead of time (but didn't, and yet responded even in order of my list). All the people I met, whom I didn't even know existed, offered me, altogether, a full view of a very secret world: rural healers, rural herbalists and farmers, contemporary herbalists who trained with elder Mediums, contemporary witches, secret path members, museum directors, Italian writers and researchers with specific specialties and studies on the witch hunts and esoteric studies and local pockets of folklore and traditions, along with artists, locals, and the perfect people to translate for me all the many dialects of the people I'd meet in various countrysides and villages and regions. All the transportation I'd need, all the extra Italian and American books that helped connect the dots, and things like money and opportunity, all appeared to support this journey and tell the stories. Significant villages I needed to visit to not only feel the resonance of, but to hear local stories I was connected to, all sorts of insider experiences I had no way of knowing existed or were possible were brought to me, access to ancient ruins off the beaten path were given, as if a path had been created and now everyone was inviting me to the journey.

The people living the lifestyle I'd be writing about in what became my first book "Italy's Witches and Medicine Women Vol 1" were the most important part of this journey. They showed me rituals, cures and traditions in action, but it was difficult to understand the full scope of this without all the periphery learning, because these traditions aren't written down, and they are part of a larger whole, and much of them are based on an understanding that is difficult to put into words.

The practitioners don't speak much about the inner-workings, and those who did with me used a language style that made sense to them. Spiritual ideas are difficult to express, and in written documents throughout time, the styles and ways of trying to express them change. If you know what to look for, you can find them (their roots, the appearance of structure, the components) and the language and style don't matter at all. But most people look at the surface rather than the ingredients and miss everything. On this journey I was given ingredients, inside experiences, outside diagnosis, I also took healing cures, visited the mountains and homes, plucked the plants, took the remedies, learned the hand signs. This was much bigger than myself, which I didn't realize before I went. My goal for this trip was a personal quest, but it began to grow beyond this before I even flew to Italy. And after arriving, I was made a custodian of information that was meant for people beyond just myself, although I acquired much more for myself and my own personal journey to keep for myself. Before this journey, I'd not been a writer at all-writing a one paragraph biography was a major struggle. Channeling changed all that.

WINGED

Since earliest childhood, I struggled with painful health issues. During the more painful times, or in their aftermath, I would just let my mind wander, searching for the meaning in this. I knew there were lessons, and I felt I just had to try a bit harder and look a bit deeper to find them. Art and music were ways of processing my emotions and building better worlds, but my thoughts asked me to face them without distraction and to seek the deeper meaning.

When I was really struggling, I would see (in my imagination) a phoenix bird near me, usually on my right side. He would show me his burn cycle and explain its benefits, teaching me how I can look at my life in cycles rather than as a linear timeline. In this way I was able to process my experiences, as a pre-teen, not just my health, but all things: that in order to become better, at the end of a cycle I would need to feel myself burn down to nothing and be born again, over and over. This is growth. And, this is how I found the song "Seele Brennt" by the German band Einstuerzende Neubauten who wrote about similar cycles.

Other than horses being an animal I was deeply connected to, wings were the animal feature I was most obsessed with, as if I were trying to recapture a part of myself that I no longer had but remembered still. I repeatedly dreamed of escaping danger by being able to fly in a specific way. It was an automatic response in these dreams, like *they* were teaching I *had* wings, not that I was creating them to escape. Because each time I found myself in the middle of a dream battle, surrounded on all sides with danger, I had to remember that I could fly: I'd always have a moment, sometimes when I was within reach of the crowd of people trying to harm me in the dream, where I remembered "oh, I can fly" and then I'd vertically lift with wings, sometimes too slowly for comfort, but it all felt very real. I regularly had dream battles, where I was protecting people from a group of attackers, or hiding people from attackers, and sometimes it was just myself in the battle, always escaping via flight.

In the 1990s, when I was in my band Crisis, my father died. I wrote a song about his death and built a large set of wings and wore them onstage when singing this song. In my imagination I was sending him off to the afterlife. Little did I know at this time that this was the role of the historical psychopomp, a Medium who does the same thing, and that this would be a role of mine in later adult life.

In 2006 as I was learning the practice of Reiki healing and learning about my psychic abilities and what I could do with them. I'd give healing to co-workers who'd get injured at work, give energy to people with various diseases, head colds, different cancers, I'd work on animals, give distant healings, all sorts of situations.

As I was being trained in the various levels of the healing art of Reiki, I was told I am just the middleman, the channel through which the energy moves into a willing recipient, that Reiki is a Universal energy, not my energy. The willingness of the recipient was just as important because ultimately I was not doing the healing, I was just facilitating it, directing it to where it needed to go, since healing is an agreement between the energy, the healer channeling the energy, and the recipient of the energy. But, 2 things began happening regularly. One, people who asked me to send them some healing energy in various parts of the world all said that I appeared to them, glowing and with wings. I would appear that way during our agreed upon healing session, but that I would also hover near them this way when they asked for me in their hospital room, or their home, when they needed support.

The second thing that was occurring regularly is that people I'd met or had talks with, often acquaintances but also some friends, began to tell me that when they had a scary dream, perhaps someone was trying to harm them or something bad was happening, that they'd call out my name in their dream and I would fly or float to them, protecting them from the danger.

In recent years this has continued, as friends tell me I teach them things in their dreams, or they call my name to help them when they see ghosts or weird night happenings, that they feel protected by my voice or my photo. Of course, peoples' dreams are their dreams, and just having a dream about someone else doesn't mean that "someone else" actually visited you in your dreams.

I've had one night time experience where I was dreaming, and all around me was just blackness, like a void. And then, my friend Alex appeared and hugged me very close and tight, which was unusual for him because he doesn't really-express emotion in this way. But I felt him in my arms, I wasn't just seeing this happen.

The next day at work I asked him what he remembered about 2 a.m. He looked at me and said, something like "I was with you." So we both excitedly compared notes: he told how he was able to travel to meet me, I told him how I experienced him. This was the only time I was ever with someone in my dreams that I lucidly interacted with, who now shares the same memories of this experience as I. We dreamed ourselves together. And while there were no wings in this flight, we did in fact fly.

ART IN THE AIR

My favorite painters from a young age were Anselm Kiefer and his dark and textured paintings, all Italian painters: especially anything with gold in it from the Middle ages, (even though I don't like religious iconography), the dark colors of the Old Masters, and Caravaggio. My other 2 favorite artists are Nancy Grossman the mixed media sculptress and Joel-Peter Witkin's photography as well as early works of the Starn Twins.

I began oil painting when I was in middle school. I was in love with oil paints and their dreamy qualities. They felt to me like walking into the darkness and finding all the treasures there in the dreamy, liminal spaces. My first paintings were dark-in color and theme. They looked like a mix between Caravaggio's high-contrast lighting along with Old Masters soft skin blending of people living in the chaotic yet calm worlds of Kiefer.

Years went by where I didn't paint at all, keeping busy with other projects. I found, however, when I returned, it was like no time had passed in terms of not losing skill, and it seemed my skills had up-leveled to match my ideas of what I wanted to paint.

In 2006, I painted a large scale series of paintings. When I completed them, I wanted to start a new series in a new style but I was struggling. That large scale series seemed to paint itself, but the new ones I was trying to paint were sometimes turning out as I'd envisioned, and other times they were not. I wanted to find a way to make all my paintings have consistent outcomes.

The problem was, I am not an artist and never have been. Artists I know spend time on their craft-they sketch a lot, try new techniques, have sketchbooks they work in regularly often making mini test paintings to get the colors or tones correct for the "real thing". I've never done any of that. I just "go" and make the idea I see in my mind. But, while I was struggling, I decided to try to learn how to paint fabric folds and clouds, for example, from youtube. It was a miserable fail for me...it's like my mind was trying to do a math equation that made no sense to it. I bought an instructional video from another artist, another fail for me. I tried drawing, it was a disaster. The only thing that was the result of all these efforts was that I felt I had no skills at all and consequently I felt repelled by painting. My husband took me out to dinner and mentioned that I didn't seem to be enjoying painting at all, and asked me what I really wanted to paint. I realized I wasn't sure. So, I took a break.

Usually I'd use some kind of reference when painting, because I always painted people doing things, so I needed a photo of myself or from a magazine as a reference for lighting and shadow consistency. During my break however, I bought some acrylic gouache paints and wouldn't allow myself to use any references and I wouldn't allow myself to lightly sketch what I was going to paint on the canvas or paper and I would not allow myself any realism...I was going totally freestyle.

What happened was a feeling of inspiration to paint these wild looking beings: shaman healers with very specific faces, very specific line patterns on their faces, and really interesting color combinations (I'd never used before) that seemed to have a specific purpose. I also made some masks with super long wig hair, bringing them alive from the paintings. I called them "The Ladies who Protect". I really enjoyed being free and not having to make things look realistic. And at the same time, these characters were very defined, certain, alive, consistent, androgynous, although I didn't plan them out at all. I was painting on large scale cotton printing paper using pinstriping brushes and it felt more like I was painting energy. 7 years later or so, I found out the types of faces and masks I made are similar to very ancient Japanese and Sardinian shaman masks.

I loved these characters, but after a time I felt I needed to get back to oil painting. And after this break I also felt clear to make a commitment: I decided to devote my paintings to witches, shaman, and healers-in-action. I got the idea to ask my Guide-in-spirit to help me with my devotional paintings. She is a sort of teacher to witches of secret traditions and I met her, in spirit, in Tuscany, Italy, when I was staying there in the middle of olive tree and grape fields of Castagneto Carducci. She had been teaching me things about healing and channeling, so I asked her to help me not waste any efforts, to make each painting count. I told her I didn't want taste time sketching, and I didn't want to waste a single canvas, and I wanted to paint things beyond my skill level.

The every next day I received a free art magazine with an interview of an oil painter who used the verdaccio technique and my Guide told me this was my key. From here we'd work together through agreed-upon signals and process. One signal was: when I felt the oil paint colors in my body as though they were moving through my veins, like I could taste them and smell, them, it meant I should answer her calling and open my creative mind. There she would place an image of a completed painting. I would take a mental snapshot.

Next it was my task to take a photograph of myself in a similar position of the person in the painting for lighting reference. Then I had to make a simple line tracing of this and transfer it to the sepia-toned canvas. For other parts of the painting, such as animals and fabric folds that I didn't know how to paint technically, she told me, "Just keep your brush on the canvas and we'll help you." I followed the simple steps of verdaccio, but most of the time I was in a trance, and the paintings really painted themselves through me.

This gave my paintings consistency, it reduced struggle, and it gave me an otherworldly experience. I simply had to put myself in the position to channel this energy, then to have my colors ready, my brushes ready, and just, as she said, keep my brush on the canvas.

If you were to look at my paintings altogether in a timeline, you'd be able to see a definite shift in consistency and technique that is tightened up. My style is recognizable in all my paintings, but since I began painting with the intention of channeling, my paintings look like they were all painted at the same time, meaning you can no longer see efforts towards development that takes place over time, rather they have "arrived" at a timelessness. Keep in mind, this did not occur as it would normally-through consistent practice, trial and error and technique study. This was an overnight change. It wasn't just the techniques that I acquired, when I channel, but also a new and comprehensive understanding of colors, their drying rates, transparencies and opaqueness, and how to layer them. This doesn't mean that I know everything, definitely not. But I ceased having to "try" to learn, to struggle or to hope that my paintings would turn out a certain way. Now, they just do.

GOLDEN WHITE LIGHT OF DEATH

How I died and enjoyed it: In 2016, I had been training as a Medium at a spiritualist community in the Bay for 2 years, then I was teaching the beginner and intermediate Mediumship training programs, which I developed, for another 2 years. During this teaching time, in my meditations at home, I was being visited by one, then another, then even more Goddesses. One at a time they taught me how to sense their energy, what their energy holds in terms of knowledge and how to recognize it, and eventually, what to do with these relationships.

At first I was shocked and didn't know who to talk to about it: these were not archetypes, they were living consciousnesses with very distinctly different energies and personalities. Some took the appearance of a form, others were colored light. They were first appearing in dramatic ways, but they would teach me in a very organized, logical unfoldment. They were teaching me history, application of ancient methods, how to bring this idea of magic down to earth in daily life, how to improve aspects of my life, and the truth about them far beyond the same simple (and often incorrect) things people keep copying over and over again in reprinting in books. I kept these experiences to myself, documenting the details.

Positive things were happening as a result, in fact my Mediumship improved and my intuitive ability became even sharper, and there was the general excitement of "Is this real!?" having these very palpable Goddesses introducing themselves to me and teaching me, and my days full of wonderment, but it was still a bit overwhelming. I didn't really know anything about Goddesses. What I found in books was people talking about "archetypes" and copy-and-pasting the same information about symbols and accessories and biographies that seemed stiff and weird. My experience was that these were real, living consciousness, not concepts nor ideas. Mostly I found that many people write about Goddesses in the same way people write about God: from a very human perspective, as if the humans are creating the idea of who the Divinity is and how they feel and behave, which seemed incorrect to me.

I reminded myself that they were communicating with me in exactly the same way that all the other people in spirit do, and the method is consistent, so this was not outside of my other experiences, this communication is not different, other than it being of a broader perspective, specific in its knowledge, there is no aberration here: so if this method has proven to be accurate and true for spirits of peoples' grandmothers and friends, then it has to also be accurate for these Divinities.

I was very familiar with other types of Guides and Helpers-in-Spirit as well. But these female Goddesses were very different indeed, and their energy was much more powerful and palpable. While I'd always been amazed at how much information, even technical information, other Guides would give me, these Goddesses seemed to be bringing ancient information to life for me, so instead of just telling me things, they would tell me things and *then* draw an experience of people, places and things to me that illustrated what they were teaching, in real, earth-time.

Eventually I'd be connected to evidence proving all they taught me was true, no matter how far back in history they took me, no matter how imaginary some things seemed, no matter how skeptical I felt. I was downloading a tremendous amount of information about history (which I was completely uninterested in previously), biographical information about these Goddesses (whom I previously had no interest in), ritual ingredients, philosophy and more.

My students commented during our class exercises that they could see 5 super bright white feminine beings behind me. These beings were so powerful that some students would have a difficult time standing in front of me because the energy would make them sway, it was a very fast, bright frequency and strong enough to be felt in the physical world. Their energy was also very uplifting and expansive, and created a most loving feeling.

Not long after this period it was time for me to leave this place and take my spiritual journey where it was leading me. It was leading me to record an album and then take travels in Italy. And then, as one of the Goddesses, the most ancient one, was making herself known to me through various meetings where I would feel her knowledge, the specific vibrations of her energy, her interests, the healing power she had and its targeted uses, I left my body.

This was not a death like when my physical body was suffering at the age of 12, where I'd lose much of my experience in the ethers, among the life-saving procedures of the hospital and all its noises and panics. This body departure would overcome me in a most glorious and otherworldly way, most delicious and beautiful.

I found my vision being blinded with light: white, gold, yellows. At first it just glowed around me and I thought perhaps the sun was coming out from behind a small cloud, but then all I could see was this golden glow. Then I started to feel warm and tingly. It reminded me of when we say we "fall in love" with someone, those moments when we credit all those tingles in our body and cells to the way this other person makes us feel, and time falls away and we feel electric and more alive than ever. I felt this, and I felt it even more in all my cells, as if I were receiving an energy attunement, so strong that I felt alive in ways I've never felt alive before. I felt totally turned on by life, and for no apparent external reason. I was in love with be-ing, not because of someone else. I felt suspended in an orgasmic state with no conclusion. I was losing awareness of my limbs, my torso and I was sure I wouldn't be able to walk, and I might be in danger if I were to lose consciousness in public, so I knew I needed to lock the door and lie down before I lost total control of myself.

And then, I fully passed out of my body without any pain or illness, and I found myself, mind intact, without any sense of having limbs, in a place of blinding light. White, gold, yellows. I had no sensation of weight, so it wasn't as if I were floating, I just was here inside the light, I was also the light. The light looked a bit like sacred geometry, a bit like those vertical numbers that move in the Matrix movies, and very difficult to describe, because there was so much imagery of color and shape and glimmering and glistening but at the same time I was part of this imagery that was everything in the Universe.

I was aware I was conscious but there was not the usual sense of space between me and another person. I could hear countless voices and other sounds, at the same time it was completely silent compared to earth sounds, because here the sounds were colors, they were frequencies of light. I was aware I had an individuated sense of myself but I also felt the consciousness of everyone I knew at the same time and yet could differentiate between us with just a quick shift of attention. If I wanted to hear the voice of a friend, I just had to focus and their voice became louder than the rest. If I wanted to feel a friend, I just had to focus and I could instantly feel them.

I was deeply aware of love, both human conditional love and unconditional love, and I was deeply aware how precious physical life is, despite all of my frustrations and clumsiness and complaints, because there are sensations we can only have while embodied in physical form, such as the profound feeling of touch of a hug, of a lover's skin against ours, of a kiss of the neck and fur of a cat or other pet, of looking into the eyes of your beloved, of sharing smiles and laughter, of human scents, of feeling someone's breath near your ear, of the textures of food...and earth's nature: the mountains, flowers, sun and moon, it's soft grasses and misty rains and sounds of leaves dancing with the wind. This is poetry created by our minds and brought into physical form. There were no valleys and rivers in Source. These are things we can only experience in this limited, embodied form, perhaps the most precious feeling being vulnerability. And while in the light of Source, that love is enormous, physical embodiment offers a precious and tender intimacy that is particular only to physical matter.

These sensations are just like a full body orgasm-the climb, not the pain, not the striving, but the opening and electricity and expansiveness when you can really be in the present moment so completely that you forget your physical body even though you're responding to physical touch. This is what being in the Light is: ecstasy. I realized this is the sensation written about referring to the cults of Cybele, for example, and how people who were not very self-aware could easily be swept up into frenzy as a result of these sensations. But for me, it felt like a tantric never-ending climax that was not the result of any external stimuli...it was simply the ecstasy of life.

=

This taught me that what we think is "falling in love with someone" is really about falling in love with an aspect of ourselves that comes online in the presence of someone else who is coming online in self-love through our Souls.

Love is the key to connection with the Universe. So in these occurrences, we are recognizing ourselves as capable of Universal love, simply feeling someone else's Soul and being in love with life at that moment Soul-to-Soul. Because in these beginnings we are also very accepting towards the other person, in ways we lose later on in the relationship as we move deeper into the human side of our experience. But at first, we are both experiencing and expressing unconditional and Universal love.

Most of us instead think love has to do with the other person, but human love cannot possibly offer these unconditional and expansive opportunities and that's why they dissipate in every relationship. Most of us have at one time thought love exists in the other person, which is why we can lose ourselves in relationship (romantic, familial, etc).

Spiritual work is the work that can help us shift into our Soul space, into the presence of Unconditional love with practice. And, this ability to channel this unconditional love allows us to be more-than-human and do amazing things such as healing, helping, creating, overcoming, and things we have difficulty doing just by our human selves alone.

For me, after this particular death, not only would I become a trance channel, but I'd also experience surviving on sunlight (no food, a tiny amount of water) for a day at a time on several occasions. I never thought this was a real possibility, but it was given to me as an experience. It was also while I was active during some long days of events I was giving: driving, giving a trance, healing...and my energy remained constant all day and into the long night. I was clear, light, and I felt ageless, certainly better than I had in years!

OUT WITH THE OLD IN WITH THE NEW

Growing up, I had a recurring dream that my parents had died. The dream didn't include the "how" or "when" but just the knowing that I was on my own and free of my home.

In the dream I always find myself wandering in the desert at night time. The moon is out, and under its light the desert itself looked deep ochre red, sepia and black in the night, with many stars twinkling in the inky dark unending sky. I love this feeling of openness and eternal space out in nature in the night, both of the land and of the sky.

After some walking and enjoying the spaciousness I came upon a group of musicians playing guitars around a fire. They took me in and became my family.

In spring of 1993, I auditioned for Crisis and they asked me to join the band. A few days later, my housemate on Peck Slip was throwing a large party for many musicians from the NYC noise scene, a slew of artists, and my new bandmates. It was my introduction to the NYC music underground and art scene. As I was hanging my black and white photography on the walls before the party, my mother called to tell me my dad, who had been preparing to come visit me, had just died.

DREAMING OF WHAT'S TO COME

My first band and I would move to Los Angeles as 1999 was turning to 2000. In the year or so before the millennium, I began having intense feelings of dread about the neighborhood I lived in. I lived in a 3 story apartment loft building at the corner of Water and Wall streets. I couldn't put my finger on the pulse of this feeling, but I was happy to be moving to Los Angeles-well, I didn't want to move to LA at all, but I was happy to move and be relieved of this stress I felt every day. It would only be a few months earlier than this that I would start throwing away documents, as I do when I prepare to move somewhere new. And, though the band was wanting to make some new changes, I felt we should also be grateful for what we had already, because at any time the scene could change and we wouldn't have it anymore. I repeatedly saw images of CBGBs club in my mind and felt our time there was limited. Not long after we moved, CBGBs would close it doors forever.

Before we moved, I was working at a record store in the west village. One early evening at work we all heard on the radio that someone tried to to blow up one of the the World Trade Towers. No one was sure how much damage was done at first, all that was reported was that something blew up in the basement. It was a terrible feeling in general, but even more for me because I lived down there and hoped my apartment and cats were ok. It was only a van that exploded after all.

After that, and until my band would move, I would have recurring dreams that an alien space ship crashed into the World Trade Towers, bringing destruction and spewing powder in the air. In my dreams there was chaos on the street, the buildings were destroyed. We were in my apartment when it happened, and my main concern was gathering my cats into a carrier. Then we all had to go outside with debris everywhere, trying to cover our mouths. I remember it felt like breathing powder. We were forced to cross the Brooklyn bridge along with a huge crowd of panicked people.

When we finally got ready to move, I began having a new recurring dream: that my youngest cat would die. He started behaving differently at night, sleeping with his belly and arms against my back, which he had never done before. Usually my other cat slept at my side. And, at the first 5 hotels we stayed while touring across the country towards LA, there was a cat in the parking lot outside our window watching me each night who looked exactly like my cat. He was always in the same position, watching me. I knew what this meant and there was nothing I could do to stop it. And, after eventually arriving in LA, my former housemate told me my cat died.

After moving into our apartments in LA and while working at a shop on Melrose Avenue, I found myself becoming nostalgic about the buildings in NY and wished I'd have taken more pictures of them. This happened for a few days in a row. I was not generally a nostalgic person about places I'd lived, because I never really felt at home, and I generally don't look back at my past much, so this sudden nostalgia was out of place. It turned into a slight panic too, a feeling that I'd not see some of those buildings ever again. While I loved living in NY, I also had started to hate the aggression and lack of personal space there. Plus, being sexually harassed daily was exhausting. The was exactly one week before the planes flew into the towers.

On my day off of work in LA, on September 11, my cat Ernie and I were just relaxing on the bed, when suddenly I heard a super strange answering machine message from a former NYC housemate shouting at me to turn on the tv. And there it was: we were watching a surreal scene of the tip of Manhattan island covered in smoke where the the towers would have been, and my former neighborhood enveloped in smoke. I had a distinct feeling this was the start of ww3, but that this would be a slow, steady war that would find the world forever changed.

Later that day I would see news footage of people being forced across the Brooklyn bridge, just as in my dream. This included our former roommates still living in the loft. My former apartment stoop was shown covered in ash, firemen exhausted and sleeping on its stairs since it was one of of the few residences there, next to an Irish pub that was feeding the firemen, giving them a place to sleep and offering fluids on the news and in Time magazine. The side-streets that I used to walk every day were all covered in ash and debris from the towers, looking like a strange white-out.

=

Before the New Orleans hurricane Katrina hit in 2005, my band was booked to play a show there on a tour we had planned. I remember the night before it hit, I was watching the news with a bandmate, and the scene on the screen was of cars leaving the New Orleans area by night. Lots of red rear car lights, not so much traffic was moving, and there was rain hitting the news camera.

I suddenly stood up and told my bandmate that we wouldn't be going to New Orleans for our show, and that we wouldn't be going there ever again. I said that NOLA wasn't going to be the same. He said that I was overreacting and pointed out that the Mayor was saying on the news that they might not get hit, that he was suggesting the evacuation just to be safe. But I believed the urgency of my premonition. In fact, the hurricane hit, my band did not play that show or the other ones in that area, and we never made it back to NOLA.

Both my arrival into the band loft and departure from it were marked by deaths that offered new beginnings and of course, offered their respective pain. Rewinding to 1993, when I'd join my first band, shortly after my father would die and soon after I'd move into the band loft.

Years later, I was still grappling with guilt over his death. I felt I should have been able to heal him somehow (though this is nonsensical-I had no healing ability then, and my family didn't talk about illness or death, so I didn't really know how my father was doing). The path towards his death was a bit gruesome: he holed himself up in our basement (which was haunted) and was taking a lot of water jugs down there. I later found out he had diabetes and was trying to cure himself. But he ended up being taken to the hospital with gangrene and it was necessary to amputate half his foot immediately. It never properly healed, so his prosthetic also didn't fit right, and he had a sudden heart attack one winter morning while preparing to drive his sister to her job. I visited him not long before his death and saw a trail of little blood spots on the floor during a late night bathroom pee. I figured it was his foot, but I didn't know how to bring up the subject. Plus he seemed quite happy and I saw some natural diabetes food books in the kitchen. I told my mother and she's the one who told me his prosthetic didn't fit and he wouldn't get a new one.

After his death, I felt called to vitamin stores to read their books on natural healing. I was guided to many herbs and tinctures that were helping heal my own conditions. I studied ravenously, whatever I could get my hands on. These things were not so accessible to poor people, or people in general in the early 1990s.

Then I had a dream where he called me on the phone and explained his death to me. In my dream, I had found some natural cures and he agreed to let me treat him. He began to heal, and I was so happy that I was helping him. But in a strange turn of events he began to get tumors on his face. While they were still growing I was shown a big, dark lake of still waters. All around the lake was dry earth of terra cotta red and deep mustard yellow. On one end as a diving board, the tall one you'd see at public pools. My dad turned and climbed up the ladder and dove into the still waters, drowning himself. He told me that it was for him to die, there was nothing I could do about it, and to let go of my guilt.

FEELING OTHERS

Two days before the Fukushima reactor exploded, my husband and I awoke to a feeling of great depression. We asked each other where this was coming from, because we had no reason to feel sad nor depressed. As soon as we started asking the question, the feeling lifted. We felt it the next morning as well, and lifted it in the same way. Then we saw the news and found out about the Fukushima disaster, and we realized we were feeling that event.

I wanted to send Reiki to the people of Japan, but I had to go to work. So, on the bus ride to work, I lightly closed my eyes and intended to send Reiki to help. Suddenly, I found myself out of my body, flying over the country of Japan. I could see the shape of the island perfectly outlined and I was surprised to see its shape in all the details including topographical colors, dimensions, water waves. I was high up in the sky hovering over Japan.

I was so shocked to experience all that, it took me a bit to remember that I could look around me horizontally. So I did look around and was also surprised to see thousands of what I'd describe as Angels: bright winged humanish looking beings who were glowing a hot white light that became more golden towards the center of each of their forms. They were gathered in an enormous and layered circle around Japan up in the air with the clouds.

I'd never before experienced anything like this-I wasn't just seeing impressions, I was there, in the sky. I joined them sending energy, then closed my session so I could get back in my body and go to work. Somehow I easily came back into my body. The reality of the bus around me was startlingly dingy compared to where I had been, and I was also a bit surprised that happened considering I never felt safe on this bus.

At work that day and for the next several days I also felt the panic and survival instincts of the people, though I didn't realize it at first. I went into my own state of alarm: I was constantly waiting to hear of a disaster striking. I was on alert at work, ducking here and there as if I thought something heavy was falling on me.

I was wild-eyed and on edge, waiting to hear some kind of siren sound that happened in movies when bombs were being dropped on a city. I was buying dried food and supplies after work for our own disaster supply. My husband worried if I was feeling a premonition of something or if I was just feeling the people. I was worried that I was losing my mind a bit.

After the next few large-scale natural disasters around the world, I experienced the emotions of the large groups of people involved, so I was able to learn, with each disaster, how to discern what emotions didn't belong to me. But this first time with Fukushima, I really felt such a strong terror, panic, loss-of-everything feeling, and I learned how to differentiate myself from the collective.

=

Feeling thoughts and emotions of the collective is not unique to me. Many older ladies in Italy, the ones who were healers, told me they felt headaches before earthquakes and before other natural disasters. And likely YOU feel more of the collective's thoughts and emotions than you even realize.

Our thoughts and emotions are very contagious. After all they are energy, not physical matter, so they move quickly and are connected, as energy is. And we are not just physical matter but also energy, and our soul body and all its psychic senses are permeable. Imagine that all the air particles in your bedroom and neighborhood and state are also energy. Where is the division? At that little level, not much. It's possible that at any given time that you're feeling emotions of others. This is something we all already do when we're talking to friends, meeting up with lovers. We know good vibes or bad moods, we can sense this, but we tend to compartmentalize this with "what we see", mistakenly thinking who we see is connected to what we feel, but truth is, energy is everywhere. At any time you could be feeling the fear of the collective or the love of the collective. The terms "mob mentality" and "herd mentality" are used to refer to a mentality that has taken over a group, where there is no longer individual thought but it is instead replaced by a collective thought.

People also know how to place thoughts and energies into the collective. It's possible you've felt messages of fear "in the air", not knowing why you suddenly feel afraid or anxious. This is one of the reasons.

So it's also important to learn how to clear these messages out of your energetic space, so you're not going along with someone else's program of what they want you to think and feel. When you're not really sure how you feel about something first, you can be sure you won't exactly know how you feel about something someone else is asking you to believe, do or think. The more clear you become about how to *feel* about things, your own true feelings and responses to people, places and things, despite what anyone else around you feels, the more clear you become about the beliefs you hold, and whether or not they were inherited from someone else or if they are authentically from within you.

TUXEDO

I had always wanted a cat, but I was allergic to almost everything as a child and cats were part of that list. But when I was living in NYC, despite all the chaos of my life, I felt a deep yearning to get a cat.

In 1993, as I pressed this yearning into my mind constantly, calling out for my cat to find me (because it seemed impossible to buy one) an artist friend's friend had a landlord who's cat had kittens and I was invited to come take one. That's when I got Ernie. He was a hell-kitten, terrorizing me at night, getting into all the dangerous spaces, he was fearless, and he was amazing. He quickly grew into a very elegant and super sharp black and white cat, and he was more than a cat: a person in a cat suit. His handsome suit was a thick sliver of white at his 3rd eye, white chin and belly, whit paws, pink toes, black everywhere else.

When I was living in the band loft in NYC, he would greet people who came over the the apartment, giving his approval or disapproval, which was really a part of how we was always managing the energies of my space during the day, as well as my space during sleep. He was very gentlemanly as a young adult, so after he greeted people he would make them feel comfortable...teaching the shy ones how to play fetch with him, calming down the nervous ones. He was really good at reading people, and really good at making me take note of people who were hiding things. It became really clear that if Ernie didn't like you, you were up to no good.

When I returned from Italy with my husband-to-be in 2009, my cat would start expressing some new habits. He was training me in specific ways. He's always been a healer and helper. For example in the past when I had really rough asthma attacks or heartbreak, he would lie next to me and put his paw on my shoulder like a person would, or he'd lie on my back and purr to relax my lungs. But he was about to teach me and organize my schedule in new ways.

The new habits of Ernie began after a wild walk my husband and I took during what would be a magical afternoon. We were walking through Berkeley and Albany's little neighborhoods with tiny houses and pretty gardens, wondering where we fit into this world. We were looking at houses and imagining owning one-which one would we want? Everything looked so normal, and while some homes were appealing it felt like we were not a part of that world.

We turned the corner onto what seemed like another typical small street of the area and were stopped suddenly in our tracks- there, in front of us, towering over the other homes but also somehow inexplicably hidden by trees was a giant Victorian home which was in super fantastic shape. It had a lavish front garden, very Addams family, with full flourishing low palm trees, ferns and other trees and a black iron gate. We could see, peering through the gate and down the driveway there was a rounded glass greenhouse attached (just like the house of the movie). It was absolutely amazing, and as we looked up at the tower on its left with the little window, suddenly the Witch teacher spirit I met in Tuscany, Italy (queen of the witches) was pressing her energy against my chest and I felt an electric expansion in my heart that was immense, as if giant hands were opening my chest and filling them with light of the sun. I also began to cry with our reunion, sob in fact. He felt it too, so we went to eat sushi to celebrate that she was with us. I cried tears of joy the whole time, and it must have looked strange to our waitress, smiling and crying and laughing...and trying to eat.

After this, Ernie seemed attuned to my teacher Guide spirit. Previously he had never been interested in my "things". He loved to play fetch and string, and he loved to twirl around a chair we bought him as I'd tease him with feathers, but he never got into "stuff". Now he was guiding me to find my house keys or some other object I'd misplaced. He'd lead me to my computer when I also felt prompted to do research on my Guide and Italy, after which sometimes a singular word would pop up on a blank screen like "divinity". He'd prompt me to take dream naps during which he'd sit by my head, guiding my dreams. It was my duty to hold up the covers in a little cave shape from which he'd watch me. I had instructive dreams during these times, dreams of clarity, important premonitions or other discoveries, or perhaps my headache was healed: in some way I was always regenerated, and when I'd wake he would turn away from my 3rd eye. My husband also told me after the dreams he also had to turn away from my 3rd eye because it was painfully powerful in those waking moments.

Ernie began to take little naps at my side during my study times, which was not normal-he was a very active cat and loved to play with me. My Guide seemed to put both my cat and husband in nap time when she wanted me to study. Occasionally, If I had dropped off my meditation practice, Ernie would pull a singular book (related to my Guide) off my shelf to remind me to connect with Her. He also comforted nervous Reiki clients who came to my apartment for healing.

Next came Ernie being my Mediumship manager. Whenever I was doing spiritual work that was "safe" (meditation with Guides and Higher Consciousness, studies they directed me towards, inspired writing, painting), Ernie would assume the donut position of happiness (cat curl, belly up) and take a light nap and give me the space that my Guides needed to hold my attention in. However, whenever there was serious work to do, or if my attention needed to be on something urgent, like a ghost or negative energy, he would be on alert and in shepherd dog mode, getting my attention with his eyes and then leading me to the place in the apartment where the ghost or negative energy was, that I could then feel in my body and make a plan to do something about it. I was able to tell if I was successful or not based on his relaxation or alertness. There was a time, as I was learning, that I would use Reiki symbols to trap a ghost in a particular room, or to keep it out of my bedroom, while figuring out how to help him/her/they and move them on as fast as possible. Ernie would always watch, so I could know as a back up to my own ability to sense, by watching him, if the ghost was staying where I demanded it too (and yes, it always did).

When there was a lot of ghost activity, I'd check up on Ernie using remote viewing while I was at work. A few times I saw him keeping a ghost in the corner near the front door, preventing it from moving around. I'd then banish the ghost when I got home from work.

Ernie also worked as a mediator when my husband and I got into arguments that weren't resolved right away. Sometimes we'd take space from each other in different rooms, but when Ernie decided enough time had passed, he would come get me where I was and take me back to my husband to talk things out.

When Ernie passed, he was just a month and a half shy of 21 years old. It was right around Halloween, and I read a traditional seasonal witchy story to him, which I did every year since meeting my Guide. As I started reading, I knew this would be the last time by the way we looked into each other's eyes. I had taken him to the vet and despite his very recent old-age cat checkup not showing anything, this time she said he had an inoperable tumor and we should enjoy this last week or two he might have to live. I wondered during that vet visit if I should put him down asap, but the look of betrayal he was giving me told me this was not the time and he'd let me know when the time was.

I prayed to my Guides that he would die peacefully in his sleep, but they told me I must go through the process very consciously. I was worried: I didn't want him to suffer. Despite the fact that I was living paycheck-to-barebones paycheck, I took a week off from my job so I could stay at home with Ernie. Each day I made sure to tell him my favorite memories, I asked for his forgiveness for some things, and I reassured him he was free to go when he needed to.

I'd felt this was coming for the year prior. And I have to say, when it was just before this week I took off, so many people gave me unsolicited advice. At my spiritualist school, people told me to make sure I'd released him and let him know he could pass whenever was good for him-but none of these people bothered to ask me if I'd already done this and to what depth. It's always a bummer when spiritual people have bad ethics, some of them always looking for someone else to instruct to give them purpose.

    I was staying with a friend and her 2 dogs and cat at the time of Ernie's death. At the end of the week I took off, I woke at 5am and saw Ernie on my belly looking down at me. It felt like he said it was just about time. At work I thought about him all day, and I thought about the other things I'd need to get back to workin on (strange way our soul moves us forward right before a wound occurs). After work, I returned home, and Ernie immediately got on me and let me know "Now!" While he entered a coughing fit, I scooped him up in his bed and my friend drove us to a vet a few blocks away. By the time we got there, he was surrendered in his body and he pretty much gone as she administered the injection.

    It was brutal. No amount of preparing and thinking can get you through. So we both cried all the way home, and then I just laid on my bed, crying that night. Both the dogs and the cat came in my room (they never did without my permission) and got on my bed (which is something they were never allowed to do) and they all 3 laid across my body at my heart and belly, just silently comforting me.

    I took a long bath later that night, tears streaming down my face and neck, but then Ernie appeared on the edge of the bath, already looking so happy to be free of his body and in spirit. I had gathered his toys and crystals into a little owl bowl that my friend had bought me...and all night long he played with his toys, jingling the little bell and moving the things crystals, string and fabric mice around, trying to reassure me that he was fine.

    Each night on the train home after work for weeks thereafter I would openly sob, just letting the tears run down my face. Each night prior to that night I had hoped to get home asap to see Ernie, feed him, and comfort him. That last year of having to work and not spend as much time with him was rough, especially losing time to the trains. So now, all the memories and tears would return each night on the train. People were kind enough to leave me alone, that or I looked like one of the many crazy people in the Bay.

    When I received his ashes from the vet, they were in a beautifully carved wooden box. I took the box into my room and laid down on my bed, with the box on my heart. Each dog came on the bed and touched the box gently with their chins and then laid down across my belly and legs, and the cat did the same thing. They were very gentle and were paying their respects. They knew.

REMOTE VIEW

I arrived at work on a day in 2014, and I walked into the break room and found a coworker crying. She had recently moved into another apartment building with her girlfriend and told me that apparently the building was on fire.

Her partner had just texted her that she was alerted suddenly by the fire department who'd knocked on her door and made her evacuate immediately. She had been swiftly escorted to wait outside in her pajamas and bathrobe and wasn't given time to find her cat because the fire was intensely devouring the top floor of the building. Her partner was left to stand outside the building, watching the flames, hoping the fire department could put out the fire and not damage the building with water and hoping her cat was ok.

So as my co-worker was crying, I hugged her, which took away her need to cry. This is a phenomenon that happens when I hug people who are crying: I can feel their emotion, and it makes me want to cry, but I release it. It's almost as if touching them or feeling their emotion lifts it off them. They suddenly calm down and stop crying.

I then offered to use Reiki to protect her cat and she agreed. I went to the private bathroom and connected to her cat with the Reiki energy, I saw her cat under the bed hiding from the smoke. There was a lot of smoke. I sensed he was ok, just scared and hiding in likely the safest place. I even got a specific visual image of her cat:'s appearance ginger and white.

I shared with her what I saw except for the cat's visual appearance. I trusted the Reiki was helping, but I know that someone's energy doesn't always show itself to me in the exact physical form, and I didn't want to add any stress if the cat I saw in my mind's eye didn't match her cat. The next day, I found out from everything was ok, her cat was ok, and had in fact been hiding under bed from smoke. I asked her if her cat was ginger and white, she showed me a photo on her phone : exactly like the cat I saw in mind's eye.

=

The ability to view a place "at a distance" or remotely, can sometimes allow me to see precise details about a room or a location and people in the room, and it can also be used to get a sense of the vibe or energy flow of a place that I want to go to. It can also be used to connect with people. Energy is energy, it doesn't matter whether it's a couch or a person.

For example, I use remote viewing to scan a place before I arrive there, especially if I'm traveling and will be staying there, to check if that place might have ghosts. If so, I clear the room before I arrive, if I choose to go. Or, I might scan the future to find a good month for traveling on an airplane that will offer me a pleasant, uncrowded trip.

I can use this to see where the ghosts are in someone's house. There was a time when I was at work and checked in on my apartment and saw my cat facing off with a ghost. I was able to do some work to keep the ghost at the front door area, so when I came home I banished it completely. It was in the front door area where I made it stay while at work. Or, I can help a client with ghosts that are in their house when I'm miles away.

I also use viewing to plan trips to the post office or grocery store, so I can avoid crowds, or to find a good time of the day to jog in a strange neighborhood. Or, I can scan a city I want to visit to find out if it's currently "friendly" towards me or not.

Accidentally, many years ago, I used remote viewing to discover that someone was lying to me. At that time, I thought I needed a slightly more elaborate procedure, and I used a couple of objects that were rumored to have been used by witches to determine if someone was trustworthy enough to be welcomed into their learning circle. It worked so well, I was literally flying around the guy's apartment, watching him doing something he was lying about. That worked too well, so I never used it again.

PLAYING WITH TIME

I was working retail in 2009, which, among its horrors of badly behaved adults dumping their psychological problems all over us cashiers, was really a great training ground for understanding human psychology, learning how to deal with spirit attachments and all sorts of psychic phenomena. The shop itself was haunted, and the ghosts there often agitated the customers, which was easy: this was in Berkeley, California, a town filled with the most enraged people who love to fight meaningless fights. They claim to fight for everyone's rights, but truly they just love to fight against everyone and everything except for love.

While I was working at this art supply store, I was also practicing giving Reiki healings. Occasionally, a manager would slam their hand in the register drawer or someone would have a minor accident and they would allow me to give them Reiki which would always help a little, or even completely heal the situation.

Here and there I would gently test the waters of conversation with my co-workers which were all artists and younger than I was. One in particular, a young man, liked to talk about his martial arts training and chi, and eventually we started talking about Reiki too, because I began experimenting with time without telling my coworkers at first.

There is a Reiki symbol that works as a doorway of time. I surmised that, if I used this symbol energetically over the clock, I should be able to speed up or slow down time, or at least my own perception of time. Mostly I wanted to speed up the work day so I could get home to my husband. So I would draw the symbol over an image of a clock in my mind, and the work day would indeed go super fast. I did this so often and it worked for me so well, that I didn't imagine my coworkers would also feel it. But, they started commenting to me "Karyn, I love working with you, the time goes so fast."

Resigned to the fate of working retail, my way to make it more palatable was to take an interest in my coworkers. I'm a great listener, and I really like to support the dreams and talents of people around me, because if we all succeed in doing what we are passionate about then we all win. And I knew no one really wanted to be working retail being that we were all artists.

So, eventually we started having deeper conversations about a wide variety of things that interested us. And when they started noticing how fast the time was going, and commenting on it being connected to working with me specifically, I told them about my experiment. They were so excited. And, this opened the door to other experiments.

Then, along came a day where I wanted the time to move slowly, even though I was at work, because I had a project that I needed to work out in my mind before the end of the day, and I was nowhere near ready. I was going to have to present my ideas to someone else at the end of the day but I had nothing to present. So, I decided to use the image of the clock, backwards, with the symbol, so time would slow down. It worked! I completed my ideas, but my coworkers, whom I did not tell, caught me. They came complaining to me about how slow the day was going and asked me to speed up the time!

MY MAN VOICE

When I was in 5th grade, it was announced that our school would give a play production for the end of the year. I was a very introverted kid, very aware I was different from my classmates, often bullied, but also I was the one the popular kids would come to for advice or when they needed someone to listen to them talk about their deepest fears and heartaches. I didn't have a group of friends, and I kept to myself at school.

Learning was easy for me, so I kept myself busy with more worthwhile studies and creative projects outside of school: marionette making, music, skateboarding, studying history, learning languages, making things and selling things, thinking, drawing and painting, gymnastics, ice skating, ballet.

Despite all this, when the play was announced, my competitive edge decided I had to be in the play and I wanted a lead role. There were only 2 lead roles: a female one and a male one. The female one was immediately taken, so I decided to audition for the male lead role. The character was a rough criminal type.

I was born with spiky jet black hair that wouldn't be combed down, very punk rock. It turned copper red for many years and by the 5th grade my hair was very long, super straight, and almost black. I cut it all off, in my tomboy sports phase, so I looked like a little boy anyway (and incidentally my straight hair turned super spiral curly after that cut and remained that way until today).

Somehow I decided I needed to have a growly voice to sound like a man and that I needed to use it to win this audition. I only had a half day to prepare, while at school. So I practiced my gruff growly voice in the bathroom during the day, and then I went into the audition room after school and practiced it in the makeshift cubby area against the wall of the room, where kids could hang coats and put bags on the shelf. This area was created with a soft standing office wall divider.

There were auditions already underway, so some people were watching them and some others were noticing me in the makeshift coatroom, making fun of me, laughing at me and taunting me.

But when it was time for me to read the lines, this loud growly man voice came out of me and shocked everyone. My body posture was confident and aggressive, I felt taller and like I was embodying a superpower. I, a girl, won the male lead role and no one disputed it.

The afternoon of the play production for the public came, and no one in the school had any idea I was female, until they read the leaflet. I was the talk of the town and I blew everyone away with my voice and acting ability.

=

Mostly, I competed with myself to get stronger in sports or more technically adept with my painting, for example. I was a gymnast, contortionist, runner, I loved soccer, I loved to get my hands in the dirt and make dyes from plants. Generally, I didn't like to interact with groups of people. I was good with one-on-one. So when this competitive edge compelled me to take part in public competitions, like violin and piano and other performative challenges, it was odd.

This competitive drive landed me in a bit of trouble in middle school. My school was very rich kids/poor kids. Popular kids/nerds. Very "Pretty In Pink." My town definitely had a football thing going on. Most of the guys who were big in football became failures later in life..it was the kind of dynamic where they were such big shots in school, and so were their cheerleader girlfriends, that they didn't think about moving away, and therefore never developed other skills. Whereas I just couldn't wait to get out of there, and I used all my free time to develop myself. I tried to do the same in school assignments too, changing them just enough so I could aim them towards my passion rather than just the dry textbook information that excluded most people in history anyway. I was always pushing limits. And when I was in high school I took on lazy teachers, demanded to learn about those written out of history, and called authorities on their hypocrisy.

So when the cheerleading competition was announced, I decided I would not only win a cheerleading spot to take it away from the bitchy clique of females who were always mean to me, but I was also going to have the highest score ever in a cheerleading competition. It was my idea of infiltration of the enemy.

After I decided to do this, resources magically came together to help me accomplish my goal. I didn't know anything about cheerleading, whereas my competitors were from cheerleading families. It would just so happen that a family friend's daughter, a college cheerleader, came home for a visit at that exact time and offered to teach me all she knew. So I scored some free lessons from this woman on how to do all the specific jumps and moves and the preparatory steps, arm movements and more. I didn't realize it was such a complex world, being an outsider. The part of my mind that likes to know how things work became fascinated and it was easy to soak in all of these details. I would also have an opportunity to freestyle some contortion gymnastics at the end of my audition, which I choreographed myself.

I won a spot on the cheerleading squad, and I also scored a perfect score, which the judges made a point to tell all of us this had never happened before! But then, after my success came the problem: I was now a cheerleader, and I'd have to go to practices and perform during games, which I was not at all interested in. I have to say the squad treated me really well and even made my the top part of human pyramids, a most coveted spot apparently. I absolutely disliked every moment.

=

While countless people on this planet are incredibly talented, passionate, and full of determination, I am a clumsy human. I attribute my many successes to my ability to channel, and for me, success is acquiring the experience I desire: whether to gain secret knowledge, to paint in a style I love, to do my best at some task, to learn a skill I'm curious about and use it, and to overcome limitations.

When I am channeling, I have an ability to quickly learn and know something that would otherwise require a lot of study and practice before use. I can shortcut the learning curve, as can anyone who is channeling. As a human, I feel complete bewilderment towards living daily life, plugging into society and doing the "normal" things. My human side says "I can't, I don't have the resources, I don't know how." I was taught at a very young age that life was something to be scared of instead of embraced, I was encouraged to shrink instead of expand, I was not supported in any way to "do" to "be" nor to "dream", "achieve" or even function on basic human daily levels.

Channeling helped me start my own leather business, become a singer, learn languages, be a writer and a researcher, meet people, find the resources I need, improve my painting skills, care for my health, heal trauma, reach my goals, tour in a band, know who to trust, how to seek more out of life, to know the future, how to protect myself, why dreams are important and how they can happen, how to do the things I wanted to do with no one to teach me how....It doesn't always work the way *I* want it to, or I should say, my *human* self wants it to, and it's taken me much of my own lifespan thus far to understand how it does work, because among my successes have been many more failures. This is what I call: Open Doors, Closed Doors.

Open Doors, Closed Doors is what I call going with the flow, all while recognizing directional signals and signs of support by my Guides in Spirit and the greater Universe.

For example, I may decide I want to use my talent of painting to support myself financially. So, looking around at other people, I may decide that I need to paint full-time and get gallery shows. I take some time off my job to do this, and I am able to get a solo gallery show and things seem to be really flowing, not only the opportunity to show my work in public, but also my painting skills are on point and I'm inviting some guests that are just outside of my current social reach and they all say yes. Open Doors.

The gallery show date arrives, the paintings get hung on the walls, everything is stunning, everyone shows up and the gallery is packed, and everyone loves the art. The gallery itself loves my paintings and some chance meetings might even have attracted some other opportunities for me and my art skills. Open Doors.

The show opening is done, and the weeks go by and no one buys paintings. I take all the work down, and the gallery offers some advice about lowering the already very low prices (that they'd get 60% of). Closed Doors.

Time goes by, I can't seem to get any other gallery shows. All the momentum has died down, and none of the time and money I have invested have earned me any money nor career advancements. Closed Doors.

Almost a year goes by and I've decided to move across country to an uncertain place. Suddenly I receive emails about those paintings from a year ago and every single one of them sells along with some very larger older ones. That money enables me to move. Open Doors.

Yes, I've tried to push against the Closed Doors, thinking that if I just try harder, work harder, I'll get what I want when I want it. But this hasn't been true for me. It really all comes down to alignment between all my inner world stuff, what I saw I want, my Soul, and the Universe.

ESTATE SALE

One of the things I love most about being a practicing Medium is that the learning is always happening. It's never a dull moment. When I think I've reached a plateau of learning on a subject, I'll ask my Guides to teach me more and they do, often surprising me with opportunities to learn.

In 2013 after a service at the Spiritual Center where I had trained as a student medium, my classmate invited me to drive around on this sunny, blue-sky day in San Francisco. She is a shopper. She loves to shop: stores, garage sales, whatever it is, she's an enthusiast. I am the opposite. I buy clothes once or twice a year-moving through the store of my choice as fast as possible. If I can't find everything I need in that one visit, I am bummed out. I just don't like the frenetic energy of other people in stores. I've always lived in cities, so stores are jam-packed with people and loud music. I prefer to stay away. I also don't like wasting time wandering around for clothes or things that I don't truly need when I could be creating something. Time for me is valuable in other ways.

But this Sunday, as we got into her car, my friend said she saw a sign for an "estate sale." I thought this meant a garage sale for wealthy people! It's ok to laugh here, I'm really not a person plugged into this earthly life so well and I misunderstand many things. So, I thought, "this could be interesting". There are gorgeous homes all over SF and wealth as well, so I was a little curious to see the interiors of apartments and objects therein.

We arrive at a house on a steep hill typical of this neighborhood, and we have to climb a very long long flight of stairs to arrive on the top floor. One of the interesting things about buildings in the Bay Area is that they may look like single family homes, and yet they are divided into apartments or duplexes. I have been into very few buildings that were single-occupant.

There is someone with a cash register at the door. It's gorgeous inside: glossy old wooden floors, large windows, although lots of people are milling around, I find my place in the front room where most of the decorative objects have been moved onto a large table in front of a large picture window looking out onto a wonderful SF landscape. The entire floor is a single home apartment.

My friend has already disappeared into a back room, and I decide to follow her, having seen everything in the front room. I wasn't intending on buying anything, so I wasn't holding onto that feeling of "needing" something. I was remaining detached from the shopping experience.

I came to the first room, and I saw people in an office-type room with electronics, printers, phones, cables, and I observed how strange it was to see all these strangers in someone else's work room, dismantling it. People were examining electric cables, pulling apart machines, it was as if no part was left without attention and it felt strange, like creatures devouring things.

It was a gorgeous room, so I decided to take my attention to these things instead to help myself enjoy my time: old dark wooden counter spaces, moldings, and desks. Out the back windows you could only see the deep green leaves of the trees which had grown against them, and I almost felt like I was in Mississippi, in an old home I'd visited there before.

I began to notice, as I slowly walked around the room, that whomever I got near began to hold their items more tightly and even turn away from me. The energy in the room seemed to pick up, and it was like a pack of wild dogs tearing at the meat of a precious carcass after having starved for a long time. I noticed these people starting to move faster, the energy felt like a frenzy, all greedily grabbing at things now like, "Mine! stay away!". I was disturbed and was ready to leave.

I left the room right away, and came to find my friend looking at tapestries and fabrics in the bedroom. There was another woman and her child in there too. That room also felt off, but I tried to patiently wait for my friend. People were so focused on going through these things with urgency. After a bit I realized she'd be a while, so I wandered to the other rooms, and though I tried to just enjoy wall textures, light (all the little, simple things) I noticed the same thing everywhere I wandered: the energy in the place was off. I'd expected to see people having fun picking through treasures, but all the shoppers seemed intensely protective over their picks, looking even angry or mistrustful…it was like a dreamy movie where there was a great lack and the people were hungry for something and having to be selfish to survive.

I was about ready to leave, but to kill a little more time I walked back into the front room and began looking at the decorative bowls and statues and things on the table. Then I looked out the huge front room window, enjoying the scenery: typical SF Victorians peppered among the trees in a hillside cluster, bright blue sky with a couple puffy clouds, glorious sun, and then I suddenly noted my body felt cold and I felt prickles against it and I realized there was a spirit person here! It was a He and He was very upset.

He began trying to move me away from his objects, and then I felt an old lady spirit also, and they were both so upset, they told me, that people were rifling through their belongings. The man was particularly protective of the woman, and these were her things, so they really tried to usher me out.

I realized, as people came into the room, that it was this couple who was making people in the rooms all frenetic and greedy about grabbing things, as though they felt someone was going to take the items away from them. I became upset, not that spirit people were there, but at the way shoppers were feeling the frenzy because they seemed unaware and I disliked the whole mob mentality thing. It's like being in a zombie movie..where everyone is all zombied out and then if they suddenly realize you're not like them they will go after you.

So I and went to find my friend. I told her, "Someone died here, I'm getting out!" If it were just me, I'd have taken the time to help the spirits if they wanted it, but the psychic energy of all the shoppers in the house was so dark and low, I found that part disturbing. Actually, I've always felt more comfortable around spirit people than earthly people, to be honest. Especially when we are dealing with crowds of people at an event, a shop, anywhere where people become less conscious of what they are doing and can get caught up in an energy which can be unpredictable. When people become less conscious I want to get away from them, because it feels so uncomfortable. But for my senses, spirit people can't hide their image or their true personas. They can try, but it's easy for me to see through that into the truth-I've been doing it since I was a child.

When my friend joined me downstairs she was chuckling at me, because again I told her people died there and they were freaking out about their home being invaded by shoppers. She said "Of course they died, that's what an estate sale is: people selling off property of the deceased!" Well, now I knew!

=

Mediums and psychics experience common phenomena, but in a variety of slightly different ways. This depends upon a Medium or psychic's skillset, which of their psychic senses are more open than others, their ability to perceive different vibrations and speeds of frequency. For example, I feel earthly spirits more clearly when I am in a slowed-down, relaxed state. If I know there are earthly spirits around, such as at the estate sale, I can decide to slow down my perception and connect to them or to the situation to decide how I want to handle this interaction. And, by "earthly spirits" I mean, ghosts (disembodied people who were enfleshed before), ancestors, friends, relatives..any consciousness whose role has been to live life on earth for some time. Spirits such as Guides, Healers, Philosophers and other Helpers move at a very high/fast vibration, which is less likely to be perceived in a slowed-down state. So, to connect with them, an awareness is required that allows perception of very fast-moving frequencies. One of the ways to do this is to match that frequency best we can: elevating our energy through universal love, through ascension imagery, through laughter or any expansive effort.

NEW YEAR'S DEATH

During my preschool years, those very early years where, like all children, I was in the alpha state of meditation, just absorbing things. I did have a night time ritual, one that was partly mine and partly imposed on me.

My room was the big bedroom at the front of the house with wooden floors. I loved those wooden floors and needed to be barefoot on them, they grounded me before I knew what grounding was. I also liked to sleep on them, with just a thin blanket.

As I got myself situated in the middle of the wooden floors at night, my feet towards the window so I could see out into the night sky with the lights off, my mother would make me say the lord's prayer. I didn't understand why I had to say a prayer to this man called god whom I never met. I didn't understand why I was praying to give my soul to him in case I died in the middle of the night. I thought this was very odd and asked my mother about it, was true that I might die tonight?

This passage concerned me ("if I should die before I wake, I pray the lord my soul to take") not because it mentioned death, but I felt intuitively that by saying it was possible I was somehow calling it upon myself. I wasn't sure how to express this to my mother, so I just asked her if it was possible, thinking that she would answer my in-between question, and reassure me that I wasn't going to die even though she made me talk about possibly dying every night before I went to bed.

I really liked the night time, but this prayer ritual was disturbing because it felt like it was trying to make me afraid of life. I loved the dreamy state where I could imagine things, imagine doing other things I desired, and at the same time I was afraid often because of ghosts so I didn't think it was necessary to add an imaginary cause for worry, of dying in the night. Ghosts were real, but god was just an idea, and I didn't want to give this stranger my soul. My soul was mine. So I asked her, hoping to clear this up and reclaim my peace because she made me say this every night which I found irritating. She said, instead of comforting me, quite coldly, "Yes, you might die. So you have to say this prayer so god will take your-soul." No reassurance, no "I'll mss you if you die," just plain and simple: yes, get used to it, you could die at any time, especially at night in your sleep.

I noticed she seemed excited about dying. She added a new ritual to my life when I was just a bit older. It had to do with New Year's Eve. I first was excited about NYE. How amazing I thought it was, this concept of one year ending and a new year beginning. But, at a certain point each NYE we had to go to the church and sit there in the dark with candles doing the same thing: anticipating that we'd die that night, making sure to devote our souls to god. The amazingness was corrupted.

I rejected this, I thought it was so unfair that I had to live under these conditions and now my mom wanted me to die before I was old enough to have my freedom and go after my dreams! So I started praying to the air to at least let me have sex and be able to travel before I died. Frankly, spending all my free time in the church was boring, depressing, the colors were drab, the songs were slow and dull, there was no life here.

But this perverted inheritance I received from my mother (my dad didn't participate) was one that made me fearful on each NYE no matter how I tried to not let it affect me. When I moved away to NYC for art college, I was happy to be invited to NYE parties and to go roaming the streets of Manhattan to force myself out of my fear, to force myself into enjoyment. While not a fan of big gatherings, I do like to see people happy while I'm in my solitary bubble. So the fact that I went out these nights until I broke away from my freedom, forcing myself into public spaces and private parties, was my way of undoing what my mother did so I could come to my own emotional reactions and mental conclusions. I was very aware, long before I went to college, that I didn't want to end up like my parents, so I started evaluating my behavior at a young age, paying attention to any habits I seemed to inherit from them, cleaning my mind from those and taking actions to put me into a more open state of mind and heart.

WITCH HUNT

When I tell people my mother has been trying to burn me at the stake since I was 4, they laugh. While she hasn't been actually trying to burn me with fire, it's true I have been pursued by my own personal witch hunt, and it's still ongoing.

My mother has been obsessed with god the man since I was very young. She viewed everything through the moralistic (and hypocritical) eye of the church, and it got worse the older I became. I heard a constant rhetoric of her telling me to be careful, that the devil was influencing me and I needed to always get right with god. It didn't seem to matter that I was going to church (while I lived with her, even though I had no choice), nor that I got myself baptized at a young age. For a period I was interested in jesus as a rebel figure, and I accused the church of being hypocrites for using jesus as their symbol and yet not adhering to his principles.

After I moved out at 18 years of age, in her mind I was still incapable of making non-evil choices, and she made sure I knew it in long 9-10 page handwritten letters she'd send me each year, along with phone calls telling me I needed to get right with god before California fell into the sea. It was common to get phone calls where she'd tell me I was calling demons to myself, accusing me of having sold my soul to the devil. For some reason, she thought I was abnormal, and the only thing that would help me was converting to her religion and letting god the man cleanse me and make me right.

She's never given evidence that I'm evil. When I lived at home, I never stayed out late, never drank nor tried drugs, never skipped school. I graduated early, was in the Chicago symphony orchestra when I was 13, I was studious and productive, introverted and athletic, super polite and responsible. So, she made up stories in her imagination, and she believed them . She's still making up stories and believing them, then sending me the appropriate bible verses that accuse me of being whatever attribute the passage says needs to be purged by god.

In my mid-30s, I was visiting her while she was on a religious high. She was in her righteous phase. She had other phases too, like the "seeking out Karyn's evil-doing phase" when she pretended to be curious about what I was doing at the time, but really she was trying to find where I was doing evil deeds (according to her). Then, she'd put all her mind power to work trying to stop me from achieving them (goal reaching, traveling, earning money through my art, music), targeting anything and everything involving "expansion".

During this visit, she told me rather joyfully that if god asked her to sacrifice me, she would have to, and she didn't want me to take it personally. During other visits, it was common for her to also tell me, while eating breakfast, that she saw satan standing over me while I slept. These types of things are ongoing.

This same lady, before I left for art college, didn't teach me what a bank account was. I found one in my name, sneaking through my father's dresser, and I took the money out of it. She never took me to a gynecologist, never taught me anything about my female body, never taught me any practical life hacks either. During a phase when my parents were about to separate, after my dad lost his job and my mom would spend all her time after work at the church, my sister and I were home alone, often hungry. We just had things in the pantry like dried pasta, and very little fresh food, because during this time, after my dad lost his job, we were very poor. I put the pasta in the pot to make my sister and I something to eat. I turned on the heat, and after a while I noticed it wasn't changing. I didn't know I was supposed to put water in the pot. So we ate hard pasta on more than one occasion. My father, a very tall man, had a different contribution: he would regularly ragefully scream within inches of my little face, then leave the room for a bit, and return sobbing and begging for my forgiveness.

It's a weird way to live, being pursued obsessively by someone who really needs me to be the projection they have of me, which is not a positive one. Of course, under all that is my mother's own trauma that she won't deal with. But, society supports obsessive people, as long as they look like the majority, if that majority has a habit of creating enemies and pointing fingers at them (as a way of being distracted from their own needed healing), as scapegoats. Churches who proselytize do this, and it's the church who's given my mother the perfect place to train for a war created in the imagination. This imaginary "us versus them" gives them people to proselytize to, and they actually train for this. They need real people to fill these roles. This is what the witch hunts were too, many years ago.

Oppressors become obsessed with survivors. When a person in authority or power (church, gov't, family members) pushes someone down by removing sources of income or sustenance, or by banishing people...only to see they find a way to thrive or to just sustain and not fall apart completely or in fact succeed in following their purpose or goal/dream, the oppressors become envious and obsessed: How did they do it? Why aren't they dependent on us? Why aren't they broken?

During the witch hunts, which I write about from the Italian historical perspective in my first book "Italy's Witches and Medicine Women Vol 1", I show how witches were not evil women in league with the devil. They were healers, spell-breakers, midwives, caretakers who were connected spiritually to a Divine Feminine Mother figure. While some healers/midwives/protectresses were making a living delivering babies of wealthy people, many others were unmarried/widowed, and poor. Still, they were able to access knowledge of natural magic, and this was a power, especially envied by the church who tried to make power off-limits to regular people in order for people to rely on the church for assistance, thereby losing their own power and becoming increasingly dependent on outside "supply."

As the church funded all-male medical schools who economically put themselves in comepetition with female midwives, just as church stories about jesus put themselves in competition with non-christian masculine and feminine healers and goddesses and gods who were important part of communities long before jesus existed or was created, the church needed their competition to be destroyed through anti-propaganda, to turn customers away from what they have always trusted and turn towards the "new providers". This anti-propaganda was especially important because male doctors were failing at delivering babies in the early 1300s, so a story cover-up was needed: insert stories of evil women, sex frenzied, conspiring with the male devil to control others, and voila, a perfect deterrent.

The reason the focus was so strongly on women in witch hunts is because all spiritual practices that came before jesus were focused on the regenerative property of the feminine-on-earth:the womb and menstrual blood. Prior to jesus the universe was seen as the giant womb/source of all life to which all life would return. This became usurped by masculinized paganisms in their wide variety, and turned into a masculine-centered universe, in attempt to eradicate that feminine power on earth (to give birth) and its counterpart "in heaven" as divinity, the original divinity. The parallel between unseen and seen, between "heavenly and earthly" being observed through women was a true power indeed, one that can't be copied, so in order to establish a new reverence for this regenerative power, a new reverence with a new masculine face, the old must be destroyed or seen as non-desirable with an extreme emotional component of repulsion and hate attached (and punishment) to deter people from going back to the past feminine ways.

The truth of course was that the church was sex frenzied (see the witch tortures for proof, there was always a sexual abuse element*) and the church was controlling people (poor women were not controlling anyone, or for sure they would fight back at the church to save their own lives, right?). And this is the way it has been for those with economic power, authority or the upper-hand, to be able to oppress people economically poorer (or culturally marginalized) taking a truth and turning it a little bit...so that people stop looking at the oppressor's perversion and only look at the imaginary evil creation, created by the oppressor.

*stripping women naked so they could search their bodies thoroughly, creating torture devices that pierced vaginas, christian men paying to rape imprisoned "evil witch" women, shaving bodies of naked women while groups of men watched, all of which have been normalized and never criticized by the church nor society-at-large.

The church was obsessed with women: obsessed with women who could take care of themselves, women who didn't need men, women who helped others, women who could actually heal people. In our contemporary society, the residue of those witch hunts is that people still believe in evil witch women and normalize all the sexual torture, rather than recognizing the plan was to break a person's trust with their own ability to connect to the wisdom of the Universe all on their own. It was truly an attack against our psychic senses, against nature's healing powers, and of course, against the Mother. The witch hunts were a distraction, social control.

There's strength and also cowardice in numbers, and historically strength is only about numbers (financial accumulation, people united against other people, fueled by a need for power and control stemming from a deep internal envy of otherness and repressed shame). Churches are called "institutions", and an institution is about a group-concept, so it's necessary for the institution to enact mind-melting submission to common ideas which involve getting rid of individuality (for a king, a god or ideal) so the new recruit will adhere to the institution. The institution, in turn, grants a person a certain immunity so they can act to seek out enemies of the institution and attempt to destroy them in behalf of the institution. It's to the benefit of the institution for its members to be in denial of their own trauma (or to keep the blame external) because it makes the members easier to be implanted with new ideas that will control their perspectives. The less ability a member has to think for themselves, the easier they will work for the collective, the easier they can be turned into a weapon against otherness.

From a higher perspective, it makes sense why my soul would choose Karyn's life path for what it wants to accomplish this incarnation: My soul knew I would write a book about healers, midwives and the witch hunts. My soul knew I would try to become a healer, so my soul was matching itself up with experiences that would literally bring to life dynamics of being a woman, being persecuted with religion and obsession, being treated badly by doctors, etc, so I would seek out the truth and have an inner understanding, especially since in many of my past lives I was a man. To understand the threat of male violence and emotional manipulation, to be gaslighted by my own mother, to be scapegoated for an evil I have no relationship with, to feel pursued by obsessive people, these gave me an inside understanding of "not being safe" being me.

For our human selves, we define success as arriving at a desired endpoint. But for our soul selves, success is about coming into an embodied life full of the opposites of what we seek, so as we decide to try and overcome these opposites (the challenges to getting what we desire) we can remember our unlimited potential and the Universal truths hidden behind physical reality. For a soul, going through challenges offers us growth and the opportunity to shed our smallness: self-doubt, disbelief in our worth, etc.

SURRENDER TO THE UNKNOWN

One evening I received a call from my husband who was at work. His boss was on the verge of a nervous breakdown and was unable to speak. This man was willing to receive Reiki, not knowing much about it, because he trusted my husband. They both arrived at our apartment, his boss was still unable to speak. I laid him out on our futon and my cat came to sit next to his head to comfort him, as he often did with nervous clients.

I told him about the gemstones and crystals I would lay on his body, and he agreed to have them placed on him. I told him to not worry if they fell off, because that meant they were finished doing their job. We began, and I started sending energy into his head and the chakras located in that areas. He was really surrendering to the energy, and I felt that as a sensation of his head falling through my hands and through the pillow.

I sensed there was a great disconnect between his mind and heart and that his heart really wanted to be heard and be a bigger presence in his life, to act as the "brain", but his mind was edging it out, causing mental stress beyond what he could bear. Rather than move my hands through the usual Reiki positions, I was guided to connect his head with his heart. As I did, suddenly his whole body reacted intensely: his head and part of his upper torso began to bounce up and down off pillow, and likewise his feet and lower legs were bouncing off the bed. It was as if he was plugged into an electric socket and receiving a jolt of energy! It was an extreme reaction I'd not seen before, and although I knew the Reiki energy could do no harm, it was intense! The stones flew off, he kept his eyes closed and his face was absolutely serene, completely trusting the moment, moving like a jackknife, and my cat remained near his head as well. I continued for an hour.

After the session, and in continuing weeks, he reported to my husband that he was able to sleep through the night for the first time in a year, and he felt so great he was even waking up early to just watch the sunrise and just being grateful for it, expressing to his wife how grateful he was for everything in his life.

This was a dramatic change for him and his wife was even surprised. It was as though he'd received an attunement: an awakening resulting from an influx of large amounts of unadulterated energy that brings about enlightenment. This powerful and quick change was due to his trust and surrender. I directed the energy to where I perceived the needs were, and I was offering to be the channel, but he was willing to receive it and make a huge and powerful change. Most of us change very slowly because our minds take time to adjust to new perspectives. But he was ready.

Our minds are such an integral part of our environment, and our environment is the deciding force over our genes. The beliefs we hold in our minds are ideas that we have repeated so many times that they've become part of our inner environment, and we are often not aware that these beliefs weren't even created by us, they were perhaps inherited from our parents or created on a singular bad day, and yet we drag them into our present and future by repeating them in our minds. If these beliefs are limiting, also our health will be a reflection of this and be limited.

GHOSTS V GUIDES

All spirits are utilizing their psychic senses because they no longer have physical bodies. The soul (in some ways an energetic "twin" of the physical body and its human personality*), is fully in its energetic form. Our consciousness is connected to our soul, as are our psychic senses. Our physical senses are connected to our physical brains, our physical bodies and our thinking minds.

Whether you believe in spirit communication or not, chances are you've had a ghost encounter (most of us have) or a very clear dream that feels like a visitation from a passed on loved one. In the ghost experience, this is what's occurring: psychic communication. It feels palpable, because you are built to sense unseen information (chills, tingles, presence of consciousness even of someone who is no longer in a physical body). The ghost may be doing something physical if they've figured out how to do this (turn on and off lights, flush the toilet, turn on the stove or radio, etc.), and while these occurrences are harder to shrug off, you are still perceiving actions from the unseen world (a different realm than the earthly physical one) in the world we live in with our "naked eyes."

While the subject of "'realms" is a big one, consider that there are 7 realms. I like to call them neighborhoods. There are rules to each neighborhood and generally speaking, the neighborhoods (if you want to imagine them like atmospheric layers around the planet, or entirely different places that do have some form of hierarchy) are not "all access". The realms closer to earth are more palpable to us and contain ghosts, passed on loved ones and friends, some bigger picture knowledge, but limited mobility and limited knowledge. For example, ghosts (people who haven't completed their death transition) have very limited mobility. They may be required to remain near the scene of their death, or within their former neighborhood.

---

*for example, our physical body has organs like our liver, heart, etc to move things around our body. our soul has chakras to move energy around our energy body. our physical body has physical senses, our soul has psychic senses. We gather and send information (and communication) through our senses. We maintain health through our organs and chakras.

In order to access the higher realms, growth in alignment with Source and the Laws of energy is required. If a relative or friend has completed their death transition, they can do a certain amount of travel, such as back 'n forth between their realm of learning and growing and then coming to visit embodied humans, or traveling to spots on earth they'd like to see. They don't have access to all the realms but they do have more mobility than ghosts do.

The type of knowledge available in the lower realm is an upgrade from earthly life, so for example: bigger picture perspectives that may be beyond our mental reach during human life, how everything is connected and the power of love and its possibilities of quick change, how death is not a failure, that the consciousness and its personalities (for a time) remain after death of the physical body.

Grumpy relatives or troubled friends may pass over and realize their errors in turning from love and they can make quick shifts in their mindsets, allowing their souls to take the lead. So they may offer (through a Medium or in dreams) apologies or seem accountable for their actions, even if their earthly personality was not. They also have the free will to stay in mental dysfunction (denial, narcissism, depression).

Manipulative spirits (ghosts), on the other hand, might focus on ways to keep manipulating embodied people, rather than move onto love and learning. No one gets a "start over free/reset" card after death of their physical body. We all pick up right where we left off. We all also have free will. If we use our free will against others in the spirit world, there are consequences in the form of not being able to live without artificial energy support (vampirism).

For most people, a common first experience with the spirit world is either sensing a ghost or a passed-on relative's communication (through a dream, touch on the shoulder, song lyrics, the scent of a perfume or soap or cigar, for example). The differences between "categories" of spirits are that ghosts tend to continue living in a similar mindset and state to when they died (if they killed themselves, they may still be in regret and other emotional soupy conditions and they may be lingering at the site of their suicide). Or, they may have devolved a bit or a lot. People often confuse "demons" with simply devolved, highly manipulative spirits. While relatives can be like ghosts (if they have unfinished life transition business) or, in contrast, they may be more mobile and have healed some of their issues if they have completed their death transition and are moving forward in their growth, the growth that their soul desires.

Simply, ghosts are disembodied people who haven't completed their death transition are moving against the natural flow, against Source/Goddess/God, so they need to support themselves with energy from elsewhere. Though it's their free will to go against the natural laws, against the growth of their soul in partnership with Source, since it is "against", since it's a move outside of the way things are supposed to grow, they must find a sustaining energy from elsewhere, and human beings offer emotional "food" for them in the form of emotional reactions, for example.

Guides, in contrast, are of a higher vibration than we are, and have access to more realms, much knowledge and healing energy, and have great mobility. They have dedicated their time to offering assistance to those of us learning what it's like to be souls in physical bodies, but there are also Guides who help people who've gone through their death transition. The energy of Guides, being so far away from physical matter in higher realms, is much more subtle. We often recognize their support or influence first as inspiration or synchronicity. Such as when a feather drops at your feel while you're thinking of bettering yourself, or a butterfly moves past your face when you're hoping for a sign that you're doing the right thing, maybe a hummingbird or rainbow appear after you've had an emotional breakthrough...something that makes you feel like someone was listening to you and is encouraging you to keep going.

Guides don't hide themselves behind shadows nor costumes, Guides don't drain our energy, Guides don't manipulate us nor jump on our chests while we are sleeping. These behaviors, against our free will, also go against neighborhood laws. If you're a being who resides in that higher neighborhood, you got there because of your operational system and understanding of the Universe and you are in alignment with that neighborhood. Rogues, rookies, and energy vampires are in the lower astral realm, and of course, on earth.

Working with Guides, like life coaches in the Spirit realm, can be learned, and for some people it's a natural thing they've done since childhood. For example, you may already talk to yourself in your head. Guides can add inspiration to your flow of thoughts to make them "you plus extra", as I like to call it.

Likewise, ghosts can read some of your thoughts, mostly the ones that have a lot of emotion around them. They use this emotional connection to their advantage by making you feel afraid or alarmed, to elevate your emotions in some way so they can get some "juice" from you, it's like an energetic meal for them, especially if you are scared. When you're scared you're less likely to feel secure; you shrink into yourself and give them more power over you.

Using ouija boards and spirit boxes are not a good idea unless you're someone with fantastic boundaries, an unshakable positive attitude and able to be mentally absolute with being in charge of your experience, have a good understanding of spirit communication through having practiced with your own senses and able to discern deception well. If you love chaos and messy experiences that can have negative effects, well then these are for you to explore.

Ghosts are by their very nature and circumstances: lost, sad, scared, lonely, aggressive, bullies, and in general, going against the natural flow and therefore need energy from you to keep going against the flow. Ghosts don't respect your free will, after all they are hungry. Some do earnestly need help since their lives can't move forward entirely until they complete their death transition. They may have forgotten where the "door" is. In effect, they are trapped in-between. Regardless, you must establish your rules with them, because they have the upper hand being that they are able to see much more than you can in a psychic sense. A trained Medium can help a ghost cross over so they can complete their death transition and move forward in Soul-growth, but this should be a very quick procedure.

You are built with psychic senses and have the potential to be a channel or a Medium, but it does take training. Whether or not those paths are meant for you in this lifetime, using a tool, including drugs to reach an altered state, can be a recipe for disaster, because you're putting trust into something outside of yourself.

A drug may give you a wonderful experience, but it may not, and you will have no control over this in an altered state. If you're a super self-regulating person, then this may work well for you, but if you've experienced any sort of trauma or wounding that has affected your relationships with people currently, such as not being able to speak up for yourself, getting your anger button pressed easily, etc, you're likely going to have little control. If a spirit sees you're an easy prey to get an energetic meal from, that spirit might also manipulate other people around you to "press your buttons." While you may not have verbally given them permission to hang out around you, if you've used a tool, you've invited them in and therefore have given them permission. Likely they'll do what they want with it.

Using a ouija board is also trusting a tool that lower ghosts know how to use, so you're trusting someone you can't see nor hear to be honest and make good decisions for your energy, you're trusting them to not be deceptive, when ghosts often lie and manipulate. If you haven't trained enough to be discerning about who a ghost is and what they truly want, you're leaving a lot to chance in a lower neighborhood. If you haven't trained to communicate with spirits, then using a tool like a ouija board or spirit box gives the spirits the upper hand entirely, and since you're not using your own abilities to understand what's taking place, you're also not aware of what else is going on: are they draining you, are they going to stay attached to you, etc.

A tool like a ouija board or spirit box are used by spirits close to earth (ghosts), not Guides and Helpers. A spirit box won't be able to easily register the fast vibration of Guides, because that frequency is subtle to our human bodies and to instruments like this as well. These tools can be neat "party tricks" if you're looking for that, but they don't offer a high quality experience nor any knowledge of a high nature.

CREEPY THINGS

It's inevitable that people will bring up the idea of "demons" and other scary phenomenon when talking about the world of spirits. Most people who talk about these things have not in fact met any demons.

For example, manipulative and shadowy spirits aren't demons. Spirit attachments that drain your energy and make you sick are not demons. Disembodied voices that are scary are not demons. Shadowy ghosts aren't demons. I will say from personal experience that categorizing types of negative spirits in this way is a general fail. It's like trying to categorize music genres-at the end of the day, it's all music. If you're dealing with spirits, it's all consciousness. And calling a "thing" (that in a moment of fear people often forget is an actual person) good or bad... there are many differing opinions about those titles.

More helpful I think is to acknowledge the operational choice, or the integrity of, the spirits: are they helpful or are they harmful? Do they make you feel uplifted, open-hearted, inspired? Do they hide behind shadows and intimidate you? And, are you sure of what you're feeling? This is a checklist for someone who is just learning to discern spirit activity, there are more nuances of course, along with laws of energy that all energy (including consciousness) in the Universe operates according to. There is no free-form chaos.

Many people instantly feel fear when they sense a spirit near them. Fear may be helping by acting as a warning to be on alert, but if fear fills us up, our senses won't be accurate. Being afraid may not indicate danger. Being afraid could make everything seem like danger. Being afraid could help us set boundaries. How we react can be highly personal, but the laws of the Universe are, well...universal and apply to all people, places, and things at all times in all ways.

In my experience, some religious people declare all spirits "demonic" and if they sense a ghost, they call for an exorcism when it might just be their own mother's spirit coming to say hello. In contrast, someone else might have normalized fearful scenarios because their boundaries were crossed over and again due to trauma, so if a ghost acts nice one day, screams in their face the next, and generally works to control them, they may normalize this and accept it, not realizing they have options or even think this is all there is. Others may be able to hear voices, but they believe all the lies the voices tell them, no matter how outrageous they are.

Some lonely people get to such a low place of emotion that they attract a trickster, thinking it's the soul of a future lover or a spirit spouse, when instead this is a spirit just trying to control them, ignoring the red flags such as: the spirit never showing appearance except for a fuzzy shadow, the spirit gives them an uneasy feeling, etc. I've encountered people with all sorts of confused stories (some mentally ill stalkers too). But none of these are demons.

We can make categories simple: spirits who respect the free will of all in the Universe and who are in alignment with Source, or spirits who act against the free will of others, and so are not in alignment with Source and who need to get energy sources from another people (vampirism). Generally speaking, human beings are exactly this, but in physical bodies, either in alignment or not. Generally speaking, most encounters people have with spirits are simply conscious beings no longer in physical bodies (ghosts). Along the spiritual path, Guides become familiar to people seeking assistance with their spiritual growth in specific directions.

Within this perspective, any consciousness that acts against my free will, in my opinion, is bad. I don't worry about "how bad" and I don't judge the lifestyle of the deceased person, I don't try to determine details beyond the fact that they are acting against my free will (barging in to get my attention, for example). I don't want them in my space, taking my energy and my time. End of story. Spending more time getting to know them creates a stronger bond. I'm not interested in being an open door for ghosts. Manipulation, hiding appearances behind shadows, scaring me, or even trying to get my attention while I'm doing something or when I'm trying to sleep, making noises with my electronics...these things are not acceptable for me. In my earlier days, I didn't know this choice was available to me.

I don't allow these distractions and drains on my energy anymore. It doesn't make me feel special to perceive all the ghosts in a room. These interactions don't have anything of value for me. I learned so much from my earlier years interactions with ghosts, but mostly I learned they are not the company I want to keep. I want to learn and expand, and the only way to do that is to move in the opposite direction from people who are in resistance to their reality.

I make exceptions if a ghost needs help crossing over, but then we keep a schedule that works for me, and I focus on helping them cross over quickly, because that process is not about me, it's about helping that spirit, after which both of us return to our respective realms as quickly as possible. Anytime ego becomes part of these transactions (ego as in "oh, this makes me cool, I'm going to make ghosts a part of my identity"), there is the potential for attracting low-level ghosts and experiences.

While ghosts feels scary, mostly it's because we can sense them but not easily see nor communicate with them. They try to make themselves palpable, and that feels invasive. But most of these experiences are simply of people who died and haven't crossed over. For some people, any type of perception of the world of spirit is threatening. There are many reasons, but this doesn't mean a demon is present. While there are scary things out there, most peoples' imaginations form a much scarier idea than what is actually occurring. If you're learning about these things through your own experiences, it can be helpful to notice communications styles and relationship dynamics you have with people on earth: take note of what types of people make you feel uneasy and why, which people you have trouble standing up for yourself in front of, and consider that the spirit world is a parallel to our world in many ways, with more options (in both positive and negative), so a great way to learn about how you perceive the spirit world (or might) will be related to your physical world relationships. These things still won't relate to demons.

Then we have "spirit attachments." These, simply, are spirit influencers who are trying to get an emotional rise out of us so they can "feed" off the emotion.

There are a variety of spirit attachments: some try to bully people *through* the person they are attached to...which is commonly found in narcissistic people and victim-complex types, passive aggressive types. When these types of people seem to be able to push your buttons super accurately and say something bone-chilling in a criticism, as if they had been listening to your inner dialogue that day to know exactly where your weak spot is, this is meant to get a rise out of you, and that "coordination" is due the the psychic perception of the spirit attachment, not the human person they are bullying you through.

For example, there are some christians who claim to be speaking "in tongues" of god who are really just channeling spirit attachments. Spirit attachments love people who like to feel boosted by ego. Ever been proselytized to? Proselytizing is based on a narcissistic view that only "their" way is the right way, and it's not enough to "live and let live"; instead ego says "we must have you be like us." It feels creepy at first...it's sneaky manipulation that camouflages itself behind being friendly, yet it's slimy abusive: someone's tricking you to let them talk to you and then their attachment gives them something to say say that gives them the upper hand. Then suddenly your emotions are making you feel smaller and angry or like crying...this is not god. An unconditionally loving god would not manipulate you into being controlled by someone else using religion as an excuse.

A loving Divinity would make you feel warm, expanded, uplifted and bright, trusting of yourself and feeling a value about yourself. A loving Divinity would not want you to abandon yourself to a stranger who pretends to have more power than you do. These people like to break you down so you can abandon yourself to be implanted with their ideas, which is just control, not high knowledge.

This is not god, but these are indeed parasitical spirits at work *through* the proselytizers.

Their tactics are just like the ones a narcissist uses, accessing your fear buttons and insecurities, and it's the spirit who helps the religious person or narcissist to scare you into silence or submission through saying things that sound like they are reading your mind, always things that diminish you. It's just simple psychic trickery, but it's also invasive, manipulative and controlling.

There are also spirit influencers who challenge us when we are deciding to move through obstacles that will improve our lives as we leave old habits, beliefs and behaviors behind, consciously. I call them "challengers". They try to attach directly to us, to drain us and keep up from reaching our goals and also to simply feed off of our energy as we are generating more of it by growing.

There are more types, and all are like hitchhikers-these aren't full-time possessions, even though some can be longstanding parasitic partnerships. After all, a parasite forms a type of relationship with its host. Spirit influencers can be tricksters and they are never helpful, that is, not without a price. They are working against the free will of others and therefore are having to participate in vampirism to sustain themselves energetically. The only way they help a human is to make them feel powerful or "right" but these sensations keep the human in illusion and at the whim of the tricksters.

Demons, in the way most people write about, do not exist. However, there are spirits who don't behave like humans, you could instead call them beings: they don't take human form (in the spirit world), they don't move about in predictable ways, there is consciousness, they don't respect free will, this is a different creature indeed. They don't look like "fallen angels" and they aren't "in league with the devil". A being like this has more in common, appearance-wise, with a chunk of metal. And, chances are no one reading this book will ever meet one, and that's a good thing.

The purpose of this passage isn't to teach you about other creepy beings, but rather to bring some clarity to the misinformation about demons. What most people call "demons" are just disembodied consciousness who know how to still manipulate energy on earth and affect people on the earth, from the realm of spirit. They can feel tangible, they know how to manipulate your emotions to make you scared -after all they get more of an energy "meal" from you this way, and they are just lost spirits or spirits who haven't completed their death transition. Still, they are bound the the laws of the universe, even though many work against the laws, especially free will, which is one of the reasons they look for energy to "eat". You can boss them back, if you can keep your emotional level neutral and know your power.

DOUBLE TROUBLE

In my early days of learning Reiki, someone told me that while it's nice to walk around the neighborhood giving energy blessings to what I see around me, it's also important to ask permission first to any human beings or animals because their souls might not want it. At the time I thought this was so weird. It hadn't yet occurred to me that people might not want to heal. Later I'd naturally learn that illness serves a purpose, whether mental illness or physical illness or psychic illness.

As humans it may sound strange until we learn to see life from our soul's perspective and the Universe's way of operating, but illness can serve as protection, illness can offer our souls the perfect challenge to work through on our way to remembering a Universal principle that can only be retrieved through experience, an illness might slow us down enough to realize we aren't satisfied with our current life trajectory or it might highlight that our body is crying for self-care, etc. Illness is asking us to learn to trust ourselves and our body's wisdom, or it may serve to block these truths from our minds if we prefer to stay in denial. Some peoples' souls want to learn what extremes a body and mind can be taken to through situations or vices, etc.

The human side of ourselves may have trouble digesting this, but our Soul is the part of us who chooses the human self it will guide through an incarnation. Our Soul chooses a life path, which it can see in its entirety before it chooses the path full of the specific obstacles it needs in order to have experiences that offer challenges, the perfect "wake up calls" that help us remember we can work through limitations with the side of ourselves that is unlimited. In this light, we can recognize that everyone has a Soul that is on a path together with their human self, and even if their path doesn't make sense to us, it's full of wisdom and purpose for the Soul that chose it.

So, one morning in those early Reiki days, and before I realized the complexity of illness, I was walking to a local art store. Most mornings I'd see a homeless man who walked in a very specific way, and I saw him on this morning too. His arms were usually down at his sides and looked like they may be disabled in some way due to the fact that they hung there, as though there were no muscles, just skin bags with bones inside. One was longer than the other due to very lopsided shoulders. His head leaned to one side as well, and he dragged one leg a bit. He never changed facial expression and also he didn't look around much, as though he had tunnel vision and was moving forward on a track. So, he walked down the street slowly, like a leaning column zombie.

As I saw him, instead of moving away and creating more distance between us, I realized maybe I should offer him an energy blessing (drawing a symbol in my imagination, and then sending it over to him also in my imagination). As I did, he was next to me, and his arm shot out horizontally with a clenched fist, as if it were punching away my blessing.

I realized in that moment, thinking I "should" send him a blessing was just as judgmental as thinking I should move away from him. I also forgot to ask his soul's permission, and in response his Soul gave me an answer! My blessing was not wanted, and that's perfectly acceptable because it's his will. So despite it looking like he was trapped inside himself, he was in fact very clear about what energy he allowed into his space. I'd walked by him probably a dozen times before, and each time he didn't react nor look in my direction. He was always frozen in a stare and slowly dragging himself forward.

=

For a while I worked in downtown SF at an art supply store that was in the weirdest location considering it was a corporation: on Market and 6th Avenue, basically a main shopping street usually full of tourists on one side and all the homeless druggies getting free meds from the state (who then sold and traded their drugs and ran into local stores to steal, including the art store) on the other side. It was a clash, and we often had tourists run into our store seeking help from a homeless person who was trying to rob them. There was a shooting in the back alley (where our store had an entryway door) opening week. It was typical SF mess.

After my shift one evening very close to Christmas time, I left, not excited at all, considering the sidewalk was absolutely jam packed with people: there was no way to get through this crowd without having your body being swiped by the bodies of others. And, it was the ONLY way to get to the train I needed to take to get home. The street was also jam packed with cars and some people...there was no escape.

The giant crowds had regulated themselves: there was a small trail of people going in the direction of the train, single-file, 2 people wide at its widest. The rest of the people, on either side, were going against our flow. As I followed the only walkway available, or I should say as I had no choice but to be bumbled along the trail, I noticed people ahead of me were having to pass a homeless person, a tall man who was screaming, spitting, yelling absurd things vehemently, and I could sense there was also a spirit attachment egging him on. The man was waving his arms and acting out in increasingly aggressive ways.

So, I started speaking to the attachment ahead of time, letting it know in no uncertain terms what I could do to it if it bothered me. I let it know it could either stay with its host and leave me alone, or lose that opportunity. I wasn't at all interested in getting in the middle of their arrangement, but I also was not going to be hassled.

Soon enough it was my turn to pass him, he was on my left and the sardines were on my right. As I had to pass him, he got quiet and still and said "Oh, it's you", and then as I passed, he immediately returned to screaming at the people behind me.

Many years later, knowing other techniques to hide or protect myself in a quick minute, I was walking in an industrial area of Oakland. I had left the house quickly, listening to music, and didn't take the time to do my usual quick aura protection method that I used when I went out in public, especially in unpredictable areas. I also used this method when I was in an emotional state before leaving the house, so I could be sure to keep my emotions to myself and not attract strange scenarios that were a reflection of my own stuff.

But this day, I left the house in a fun mood and listening to music, and quickly enjoying my walk on the way to my destination. I noticed, almost too late, that ahead of me was a woman who was yelling in jilted voices at everyone who had to pass by her.. I could also sense her spirit attachment, a masculine one, was taunting people through her. I wasn't able to move away to the other side of the street, and the street edge was filled with cars, so I quickly put up my protection and invisibility psychic devices to prepare. As I walked by her, instead of getting up to attack as she had with the other pedestrians, she got up, took her milk crate, and walked away from me calmly saying, "Why are you hiding?", and that was it. She left me alone and vacated the area.

FREAK MAGNET

My husband and I were on BART, the Bay Area train, on our way to an occult shop in Oakland, 2011. We were seated side-by-side in a section of the train where the seat in front of us faced us, so the people seated there were close to us, feet to feet.

Across from my husband a woman was seated, they were both on the aisle side, I was next to the window. The doors opened, passengers entered and across from me a woman seated herself, or I should say, it seemed like she seated "herselves" because was talking to herself frenetically and constantly, total gibberish, the kind of person we'd call crazy, schizophrenic and unstable. In her constant stream of babble she would get louder and louder and incredibly louder still, and then her volume would taper off a bit before ascending once again. She was also fidgety and occasionally she'd jerk her arms and hands, so she seemed unpredictable. And when I say "constant", I mean she NEVER stopped talking. I didn't understand how she was actually breathing. There seemed to be no inhalation.

I'd lived in the Bay Area at this point for a few years and, after also living in Chicago and New York, I knew better than to trust my safety to strangers, especially here, because there were so many mentally ill people out and about. So I kept my senses on her while also talking to my husband, even though he was quiet too, also keeping his senses on the situation. The woman across from him was trying to pretend everything was normal.

While there are many amazing people and situations and nature and creativity and opportunities in the Bay, there is also a very large portion of the population who are mentally ill, many of whom seem functional and perfectly normal looking...until you have to share a house with them or interact for more than a few seconds. I lived in NYC for 10 years, and when things would go down, people would help...but in the Bay, people seem to try instead to normalize crazy, or perhaps they are afraid of getting involved. On the east coast, if there was a loose cannon on the train, you could feel all the passengers mentally preparing themselves at the same time minding their business. In the Bay, people are just sitting ducks, they put a lot of trust in the people around them in public places, and what I mean by this is people are on their laptops and phones on trains or crossing the street, never looking up to see what the commotion is, never acknowledging the cars. So don't expect anyone to help you if you get attacked here, and attacks happen regularly because it's a culture that enables crazy. I do love living here for the freedom, despite this. So on this train ride, I was wanting to "think positive" but, you know, reality.

I remember thinking to myself, "Here we go again, I am always the freak magnet". I snuggled into my husband's arm, and turned my focus to what books I should gather at the occult book store. I began talking with my Guide in Spirit about which supplies I should get, and she began telling me about a specific magic rite she wanted me to learn about.

Suddenly, the blabbering woman apologized and became silent. It was the first time in 15 minutes she'd not said a single word. My husband whispered, "What did you do to her"? and I looked at him confused, "Nothing". Then the woman went back to frenetic talking, and again I focused within towards my Guide and she began telling me about the rite. Again, the woman apologized every coherently and became silent. Then told a little joke, laughed, and silent again. I immediately noticed that under that craziness was a sweet personality. Then she was gone, and talking crazy again.

So I talked to my Guide again, and sudden silence from the woman. My Guide told me to notice how that woman's personality seemed to be sweet when it was uncovered from the oppressive constant jitters and talking. Then she instructed me to see the spirit attachments with her who were using her like a puppet, and I did suddenly notice these dark little shadowy spirits. They tried to intimidate me briefly, but I called them out using a word my Guide gave me, and they backed off and then woman actually left her seat, leaving my husband and I to discuss. It was interesting because he couldn't hear what I was doing inside my head with my Guide, but he was observing the results in real-time.

This is how I was guided to understand the relationship dynamic between spirit attachments and people who have them attached, to various degrees. It wasn't my first time noticing them, but this was the first time I was learning the technical side of how this dynamic works.

=

A few nights later when we were on the train again very late after dinner, a movie, espresso and sweets, I was a little more prepared when a girl in her early 20s focused in on me. She not only locked eyes, but she started making her way over to me with wild dancing. I did same thing as I did on the street at Christmastime (telepathically telling her spirit attachment to back off, and they did), then calling my Guide to protect me (in my mind). And she went back to her seat, calmer, and turned towards someone else, quieter.

=

I diagnosed myself, out of sheer frustration and also with humor to laugh at my predicament, as being a freak magnet. I recognized that if I was on public transportation and there was a mentally unstable person, they were likely to find me. Same at the grocery store, or anywhere in public there was an oversexed creepy man who thought for some reason I was only walking on the street to offer sex. I really honed in on the details of my experiences and asked them what they were trying to teach me, I realized these weren't just weird people, these were people with spirit attachments. It was the spirit attachments who were targeting me, because they knew I'd freeze in my responses while I was sensing something else going on but not quite having figured it out. I was their captive audience...for a time. It would take me some time to recognize spirits attachment not only in the freaks, but also in passive aggressive people and in other situations.

It was not fun..they seemed to be everywhere. Customers at the art store who pretended to be interested in my hair, only to violently explode when I couldn't discount their already-on-sale $5 sketchbook. Or the older lady neighbor I had in SF who was an incredible energy vampire along with her attachments who liked to feed through holding people captive while she told unending stories and criticisms of neighbors and businesses who she felt didn't give her good customer service, which seemed to be the whole city in her opinion. Or the housemate who had a psychotic breakdown as she was losing her grip on reality, but who still insisted she was "always right" because she was a narcissist extraordinaire (she was from the east coast actually).

And, it took me a while to realize I didn't have to be the captive audience for these people. It took me a while to realize my human side wouldn't be able to be polite enough to make them stop nor scare them or argue them away. This had to be dealt with on an unseen level, which was as easy as talking to the spirit attachment influencing their behavior. Of course, when you're held in the crazy gaze of someone with an attachment who loves to argue or be the center of attention, it's not always easy to remember to talk to their attachment, because the attachments are great and distracting us with sensations of danger to try to keep us quiet.

CONDUIT

One night in 2012 ish, an acquaintance asked a favor of me through a friend-in-common: to send them some healing energy for their sprained ankle. I agreed, and immediately communicated with my Reiki guides-in-spirit to make me a conduit of healing for this person in the best, most powerful way possible. I set a time with the acquaintance through our friend-in-common.

The only problem was that I had sudden and unexpected dinner plans come up with this friend-in-common and completely forgot about my agreement, which is not my style. But my friend had been working at a place where he had a very long commute and we were seeing less of each other as a result. That night he wanted to meet up, and the commute he took on public transportation had its own ideas about keeping schedule.

He eventually arrived, and we started talking and ordering food and enjoying each others' company. Then, During our dinner, he received some text messages from her that not only was she feeling the energy, but she was seeing the Reiki violet purple light that is commonly seen during Reiki healing sessions. She got the energy she called in, and I was able to just be like a radio sending and receiving the signal while I could also enjoy dinner, because earlier in the evening I had made the agreement.

=

Energy can move much more freely than we realize, as energy moves in the way thoughts and emotions do. The ideas of time and space are human constructs: there really is no distance for energy to travel. Physical matter is also energy, just energy moving at a very slow vibration, slow enough to be seen with the "naked eye".

Time and space as related to our physical world makes us think that we have to take a train to meet someone, or that an ocean separates us along with time zones. But we can meet each other Soul-to-Soul without leaving our respective zip codes. It's true that physical matter is slow to change, but this is only because of our minds and the vibrations of energy. Our physical bodies believe what our human thinking minds tell them, but our intuitive minds, the minds of our Souls, are not limited to physical matter, even though they move *through* physical matter. Changes of perception can change the way our human thinking mind helps us or holds us back. When you can use your human thinking mind as the tool it is, and instead follow the inspirations from your intuitive Soul and the energy you recognize through your heart center, changes can happen miraculously fast, and that's all a miracle is: super quick change. Change moving faster than physical matter usually moves.

HOTEL INTRUDER

I was staying at a hotel in Florida. I got a free upgrade, and the room was basically a super large open living room/kitchen/bedroom, then a little bathroom next to the bedroom. There was a tv on top of the refrigerator which was in the corner, so it could be seen all the way over in the bed. It felt like a studio apartment.

Earlier in the day I was visiting with some people, and one of them was talking about a former teacher of theirs who had just died. I didn't think much of the conversation after it took place. We had dinner and then I went back to the hotel room.

I was relaxing in the bed, it was quite late and I had to start my day early the next day. I'm not a tv watcher, so I hadn't turned it on even once. I was just thinking about miscellaneous things as well as my next day. But I started to feel an old familiar sensation, a very uncomfortable warning feeling, and it made me think that someone was about to break into my room. So I became alerted. I tried to rationalize this thought away, because the hotel complex was serene by day, and it was quiet at night as well, and I think some people did live on the property as well. But there it was again, that feeling of needing to find a weapon or get my bag and wallet ready, to prepare for the person who was about to break through the door.

But then some childhood memories floated in and I recognized this sensation. My entire childhood I slept with the covers over my face, with just a little opening for my mouth when I felt the same sensation of a pending break in. As a child, in these moments, I would start to plan the best escape route for my family, and at the same time I was trying to keep the ghosts in my bedroom away.

And then, back in this Florida hotel, I chuckled to myself as I realized I was just feeling the presence of a ghost trying to come into my hotel room: this was the feeling of a "break in" that I sensed, because it was true-a person, just a person without a body, was trying to come into my room and get my attention. This was the feeling.

As I put these pieces together, the tv turned on and off. I was not amused and said, "Stop it." Then the toilet flushed twice, and at that point I saw a tall man with a buttoned up shirt and realized it was the teacher we were talking about at dinner. I told him that he could come back in the morning, after my wake up and meditation, and I would be willing to speak with him then. "But for now," I demanded with absolute certainty, "get out! I'm trying to relax and you don't belong here!"

Then his image faded and I no longer felt watched, and the "break in" feeling dissipated and I was alone again. The tv stayed off and the toilet remained quiet.

In the morning, he did reappear at the end of my meditation, as per my conditions, and I listened to what he had to say and relayed the relevant messages.

INITIATION

I moved to the Bay Area of California instead of walking into the ocean one morning at the literal end of 2005. Once there I told the Universe I wanted to know who I was and what the purpose of all these "supernatural" experiences were about. I was on a quest to know what all my dreams, premonitions, spirit encounters, and experiences I had were about from a bigger perspective than my own. I wanted to know why I felt presences of groups of spirits watching me when I thought about tarot or other spiritual practices, I wanted to know why people needed me but I felt alone, I wanted to know why people seemed healed by me when I didn't seem to be able to heal myself and why others seemed to want to destroy me...and I wanted to know who I was without music, who was I at my core, the very core of a human being without some external value placed upon me by others. So I screamed to the angels to help me find a way to something new and a sudden doorway opened and I moved through it quickly.

After this, whenever I'd take a walk I'd find a free book about gnosticism or buddhism, or affirmations or something that offered me teachings that I tried out and decided whether or not they resonated with me. I would also go to the local bookstore and open any book and find an answer exactly at the place I looked onto the page. It was a form of question-and-answer divination I had with the Universe, and I was getting clear answers this way.

I was not one to watch tv in my adult life, but one night I was watching a friend's tv and found a Discovery Channel program about a wiccan priestess who was a school principal by day. While I didn't find myself interested in her particular path, I was touched by how impassioned she was about her spiritual path. I realized I knew what I *didn't* believe..after being forced to go to church and seeing all the hypocrites there doing things like ostracize a couple for having an affair at the same time the preacher was having his own affair. I found that people were judging me and other people on the surface which didn't seem to have anything in common with jesus. I observed that people in churches liked a god they had created in their human image, a god who punished some people, rewarded others, and who seemed to give them the confidence to force themselves and their beliefs on others in a controlling way that didn't allow for otherness. Authority was a farce, church was too, what then? I considered that I *did* want to believe in something bigger than myself, but I hadn't yet found it.

Within a few days, I developed strange eczema on my eyelids. At first it was just a nuisance, but then each morning when my eyelids were hot and crusted closed, it became a real problem. When it continued to worsen, I decided to make an appointment with the dermatologist a few streets over even though it was expensive and I didn't really have the money at the time. I didn't know what else to do. Doctors never really helped, I was allergic to most natural remedies, so I had a sinking feeling but I tried to remain hopeful. The doctor told me there was nothing she could do since the eye area was such a delicate one, and she sent me home, crying, with no solution. She did take my money though.

That afternoon I was using my friend's computer when I found a guided meditation script online. It was meant to be used to meet my "inner advisor." I didn't know what this was all about, but I decided to try it.

I used the script and easily met my inner advisor, who gave me some advice. Then I decided to meet my eczema, ask it questions about why it was erupting in this way, and I hoped to make a healing agreement with it. I did this for 20 minutes a day, 4 days in a row. At the end of the 4 days my eyes were completely healed, no trace of redness, swelling or any sign of discomfort!

I had learned a great deal about what my body was trying to tell me during our talks in meditation and I began to use this method to get all sorts of answers to a variety of questions. It was the beginning of using my ability to heal myself in an organized way, and I found it easy to connect to: my higher self, my body and its organs, and guides-in- spirit of all types. I also realized my mind was so strong, and I knew could talk myself so down…I surmised I must be able to talk myself up as well! So I started to use my mind *for* myself rather than *against* myself.

Not long after this, I found an article for National Geographic online about ayahuasca. The writer was telling her story of life long depression and her experience traveling to South America to meet a shaman and how taking ayahuasca released some of it and she felt a great release and relief after.

While I didn't think I'd be able to handle sleeping in the jungle with all the crazy bugs (I had a friend who each year spent 2 weeks in the rainforest and I'll always remember the creatures she encountered) but I felt that I wanted to learn how to heal from shaman there. So I asked the Universe to help me make it happen, despite the fact that I didn't have the money nor means at the moment. I decided that's what I wanted to believe in: self-healing.

What happened instead is I started meditating for an hour a day. Sometimes I'd go even longer. Then one night, not long after starting this routine, I was having a regular day, and then I was getting into bed for the night. I was laying at the left edge of the bed, on my back, and my cat Ernie parked himself inside my arm with his face touching mine, as he usually did at night. He was always near my head, if not wrapped around it, which is something he started as I ventured into my spiritual path.

I felt the need to open my eyes for some reason and I saw, coming out of the far wall near my feet, a bright white cone of light, its point coming towards me. I assumed I was just imagining things and I closed my eyes, thinking that would stop the hallucination but when I opened my eyes again the cone was even more solid looking and it was near my belly. I closed my eyes and kissed my cat, thinking that focusing on something physical would stop this experience, but when I opened them the point of light of this now very long cone of light was just a few inches away from my nose and I yelled out loud "No, I'm not ready yet" thinking it was death coming to take me again. And suddenly I lost consciousness.

When I awoke, I was aware I had been dreaming that I was healing people with what I called "energetic chiropractic," which looked like energy healing that helped people make adjustments bit by bit. I also heard the word Reiki. I knew my sister had mentioned this word before, so I called her and announced, "I think I'm supposed to learn Reiki. What is it and how do I find it ??"

Long story short, I was sent, with the help of funds from friends and the Universe, to receive a Reiki initiation shortly after this, instead of going to South America. Not long after this I'd go to Italy, I thought for music, but instead it was to meet my husband and an Italian witch spirit who would teach me life-changing Italian rural healing traditions over the next handful of years, along with Mediumship and more.

So while I was still experimenting with what I believed in, it was clear the Universe believed in me. While I creatively worked with the Universe for my entire life, this was a new intentional relationship that was just beginning.

TAROT

The first tarot reading I received was in 1994 in New York City, somewhere in the east village in a famous witchy place. I had only ever been to one other "spiritual" shop but it was a bit more crystals and angels, and this one was roots and candles and spells.

I'd never even seen a tarot deck in person before. But, my friend convinced me to get a reading while she did also. We both attended Parsons School of Design and the first year was about to end. I decided not to continue at this school which, at the time, was so very outdated and full of disgruntled teachers and staff changes that made my year a real mess. I had questions about my creative life, so I thought maybe the tarot reader could give me some insight.

We walked into the shop, and it had wooden bins of dried herbs, candles against the walls, and it was a bit narrow and long as a space and unfriendly feeling. It felt like the kind of shop that you would go to only if you knew what you were looking for. We let the cashier know we were here for our appointments.

I was seated with a man in the back of the store. We sat at a small wooden table and my friend's table and reader were close by. It felt a little strange being out in the open for something that I felt was an intimate moment: asking questions about my life isn't something I'd like to do around people I don't know.

Anyway, the man asked me to cut the deck of cards a few times, then he asked me my question as he shuffled the cards and then asked me to cut the deck. My question was about music. I brought my guitar to my art school dorm room and I bought an amplifier while I was there, and I wanted to know what my future in music looked like. Would I finally find a band? It's what I'd been hoping for, and especially since I realized art school was for people who didn't really know that they wanted to do nor how to do it, I realized it was too remedial for me. The weight of his answer stunned me.

The tarot reader said, "No, no music for you," and so I asked if he meant right now, or in the near future, or in general. "No music for you at all now, nor in the future," he said. He told me he didn't see me having anything to do with music ever, and I was so disappointed I can't remember what else he told me after that. While I loved making my art and hoped to do it as a way to earn a living, music was my dream.

Approximately 8 months later I'd audition for the band Crisis, after being introduced to the guitar player/band leader through Aesop the cat's owner. I'd be the lead singer and lyric writer, and I'd tour for 13 years in that band, helping to change the face of metal music forever.

=

It would become a common thing for intuitive readers of all types to not be able to read me accurately, or perhaps only be able to discern a little bit of very earthy "stuff." It would take a couple decades to find just a few people who my Guides in Spirit would allow to give me a deep and precise reading. Mostly, my Guides scramble the signals for people, so I've received some very weird readings by professionals of all types that made absolutely no sense. My Guides simply scramble the signals because they don't want that person to know me in this way, or because I'm sometimes meant to intuit my answers by myself.

In fact, my audition for what would become my first band, was the start of using my intuition as a way of survival, socially, for me. I'd always used it before, but before my social circle was limited to a few people at a time. In my band, I'd meet thousands of people.

SUMMONING

My audition for my first band, Crisis, would also be the start of what I called "summoning" which was my uneducated word for "channeling."

The owner of Aesop the cat invited the guitarist of my future band to come over to our apartment to meet me in 1993. Aesop's owner knew I made music in my room on my 4 track because I would borrow his kitchen knives to use as percussion instruments. The guitarist came over quite late at night, and mostly the guys chatted, catching up about music and art, ignoring me. I got fed up being ignored and asked to share some of my 4 track music before going to bed. I was invited to audition for the band the very next day, and given a cassette of a few songs to listen to that night.

I went into panic mode because I'm not a musician. I channel, so I can't really "jam" . Instead I feel the songs singing themselves to me. Likewise I'm also not an artist, I don't sketch, rather I see a painting showing itself to me, so I need some quiet time to pay attention to these downloads of both music and art. In this case, I only had a few hours overnight to try and write my lyrics and vocals before waking, going to work then going to the audition.

This wasn't really expected of me: I'd learn later that most musicians jam out ideas and work on songs together (in these early 1990s days anyway). But I wanted to be prepared. I'd never feel comfortable working out my ideas in front of people I don't know.

At 2 am or so, I heard the song melodies to the song I listened to on repeat, and I wrote the lyrics: my download was lightning fast and very concrete.

The next day after work I arrived at their rehearsal space to audition. I was probably a weird sight for those guys: they were all dressed in black, combat boots, wallet chains...and I had bright red hair, mostly dreadlocked, wearing bell bottoms with giant flowers on them mismatched with another flowered shirt. My clothes were loud but I was very shy.

I was introduced to the band and, due to being so nervous, I asked them to play the song I worked on. My plan was to escape as fast as possible if it didn't go well. I didn't want to waste any time jamming. They agreed and started playing the song. I had my lyrics written on a small sheet of paper, but somehow I felt plugged into an energy source and just let loose, with all my vocals perfectly landing in the places I wanted them to be. Somehow I remembered all those lyrics and the song's passages, and I was thrashing about the room like a bird. Before I knew it, the song was over, I was lying on my back on the floor, and the bass player was standing over me, looking at me curiously and asked, "Are you ok?"

I excused myself and went to the bathroom, too embarrassed to return, but I had to...and that's when they guys asked me to join the band and they would give me the nickname "crisis."

The thing I called summoning was actually channeling: channeling extra energy that went into my singing, my physicality. Onstage I often felt like I was flying. I was in my body at the start of the set and flying around outside my body until the end. I always felt a cathartic cleansing after our shows, and due to the summoning I was also bright, confident, compassionate, a little more outgoing, and very brave, which is different from when I wasn't channeling.

Often I was challenged by other male musicians or male bouncers throughout the next 13 years who tried to bully me or test me in other ways, but that energy I summoned always came out of me and put them in their places, and they respected it, mostly.

CATCHING THIEVES

I've always had this strange and precisely accurate ability to catch thieves, even better than security guards and other authority figures. This extends to all "off" situations as well.

It started in kindergarten when I found my beloved star wars stormtrooper figurine stolen out of my bag and I immediately knew which classmate had taken it. As I walked over to them I caught them showing 2 other classmates my figurine but she wouldn't give it back. I told the teacher, who already really disliked me, and they all gaslighted me out of my figurine. While it's common for siblings to steal each others' things, I always knew when my sister stole anything of mine before I even entered my bedroom to look for the items.

This started happening when I was in public: at grocery stores, on buses, on trains, and it wasn't just limited to stolen "things" but I also caught people stealing time at work, being deceitful in some way. As a small child I knew when adults were lying and I knew when doctors were poisoning me. I wasn't even looking for these types of things, just doing my own thing and "poof" there it was.

When I worked at a record store in NYC I knew who'd try to steal cds: I could sense who was about to steal or who had stolen and was hiding things in their clothing just by intuition that would make me look at them just as the right moment, or to start up a conversation and smoothly shock them and make them surrender the items. Sometimes I didn't even know at first why I felt compelled to speak to these customers, but as soon as I started up the small talk, I noticed they were stealing and began my moves to reclaim the items. In fact I ran after one guy and tackled him on the sidewalk and took back the box set he tried to steal that I intuitively knew he was watching. In true NYC style, some bystanders saw me chasing the guy and helped me tackle him.

In my many retail jobs, I also always happened to walk down the aisle where people were stealing, stuffing their pockets, or trying to escape the store with items. It was especially frustrating working jobs where security guards were oblivious to the thieves and I was catching them every hour.

Along with this ability to catch actual thieves, I became very precise at knowing when someone was trying to psychically spy on me, or astrally traveling in my apartment. I can sense when people are lying about me out there in the collective, when they aren't physically anywhere near me and even if I haven't spoken to them in months.

At my retail jobs, I could always spot the customers with spirit attachments, the customers who would be feisty, the ones who would have mental problems, and the ones who would lie to get discounts. Retail work, and for sure restaurant work…any work dealing with the public is really great training ground for the psychic senses, or if you're just sensitive as a human being on any level, although it's also disruptive and potentially overwhelming. It's best to take it as psychological study of human behaviors. Perhaps all this prepared me for discovering historical theft, which part of my writing has found itself focused on.

Being able to perceive incoming danger or spot potential goings-wrong is a common thing for people who've had to grow up in unsafe conditions. What people mistakenly call "intuitive empath" is really just psychic fight-or-flight.

Empathy isn't a real thing, it's a name our contemporary society gave to something it forgot about, the fact that we are psychic beings as much as we are human beings. But because this fact has been erased from our upbringing, we don't know how to keep it in balance or how it works.

Empathy is not a psychic receptor, it's not a psychic role. Saying "intuitive empath" is like saying "the sunny sun." Empathy is the blown-open state of the psychic senses and aura which should naturally open and close, stretch and shrink. However, for someone who grew up experiencing trauma and who realized they had to take care of themselves, their psychic senses were blown open and they were kept open as a means of survival by the child so they could be on alert to scan for incoming danger always. It's psychic survival mode.

Empathy is a state of having no boundaries, of extending one's aura far beyond one's personal space, so they are in constant read-mode state, and actually, unethically budding into everyone's business because they are stretching their energy out far and wide to keep watch for danger from people, places and things, which causes a person to feel burned out on humanity due to blending with everyone's energy all day long. But it's the person who needs to learn how to close down their senses and regulate their own energy. It's actually their fault that they are psychically "on" all the time, but they don't know this.

So using the psychic senses (one of them being intuition) to read people only at specific times, or to channel intentionally, takes practice.

SHAPE SHIFTING

My experiences as a professional musician made it clear for me that I was able to transform my inner world through channeling, summoning, and be a better version of myself. There's no better testing ground for your skepticism than a public interaction.

But, over time, I would also notice during recordings, for example, especially during the Gospel Of The Witches recordings, my face would change shape and my eyes would change color, rather dramatically. My eyes have changed colors since I was younger, but it's not something I can predict in the way that some people know their eyes will change from summer to winter. Mine change when I'm channeling, and it's based on *who* I'm channeling.

When I travel around Italy, my face changes dramatically based on whether or not my Guides love a place I'm spending time in. For example, when I'm in Tuscany I will look 20 years younger and be aglow. When I'm in Naples, I look hideous. It's not just the youthfulness or ugliness either: often my face changes to be rounder or more angled, my eyes change their presence. I take photos of myself during my travels, so this can be clearly seen by other people. When I visit places where women were burned, my face changes to give some effect of the women who died there. I can look 20 pounds heavier in one village one day, and look more beautiful than I ever have in another village the day after. Italy, for me, is about connecting with living history, so for me it's not about leisurely travel.

This is nothing new: all the controversial documentation of ectoplasm in the 1800s had to do with this phenomena. Instant healing does as well. Platform Mediums can have this ability to change posture, facial expressions and style of speaking based on who they are speaking for. They aren't consciously making changes, they are being changed by the spirit they are speaking for.

This really has to do with the deeper magic of our cellular structure: inside each cell is a gene (inside most cells), and that gene contains instructions on how to make specific proteins for the cell and its function/needs (to power up muscles, to attack invading bacteria, etc), so in other words, the gene is influenced by its environment and so is the cell and onward until we reach our skin, which is also affected by its environment.

Shape shifting is nothing more than changing our matter based on energetic environment. And, if we are able to do this with our human minds, or with the help of higher consciousness spirits, we can change our matter quickly, or to take on an impression of otherness (healing is changing our thought and emotion environments).

When I travel in Italy, my environment changes my appearance and also my energy. When I channel for my students, my energy changes to a very motherly energy, as they tell me. When I channel for music, my energy is absolutely fierce and expressed a most ancient blend of masculine and feminine enrergy. I can channel a terrifying masculine energy. I can channel the softest unconditional love.

As a human being, I'm a clumsy, humble, introvert. But my hopes, dreams and creativity have given me places to focus on expanding myself, and this focus has blended with the Universe, and the Universe lends me energies to accomplish my goals and hopes and dreams, which are quite different from each other and need different energies to be accomplished. In this way I can create beyond my human limitations.

SOUL RETRIEVAL

One summer I got sent to bible camp. Ironically the place was named Camp Good News, and it's since been shut down due to rampant sexual abuse of camp kids by the camp counselors.

I was there a few days before camp officially started, along with small group of kids who knew adults working there. I noticed a tall blonde man and I immediately didn't like him, because he was always watching me hungrily, so I also watched out for him, to avoid him.

One day, we kids were in a room with games. The rule was we had to clean up after ourselves or get punished. The blonde man entered the room, his eyes focused on me while he closed the door behind him and locked it. I was the only one who noticed. Immediately I knew I had to get kids out of that room. So I distracted the man, opened the door, sent kids out in all their happy screaming chaos, and I was the sacrificial lamb.

I told an adult later, they didn't believe me nor help me. And I realized, yet again, that no adult would be helping me or saving me. I had to save myself. This man kept coming after me, so brazen he even tried to rip my shirt off in front of other adults. Throughout the duration of camp, I had to scan the public bathrooms before I went it, I kept my fingernails sharp. I fought him off every time, and it brought out the fire in me. That man got arrested and jailed not long after I was back home. Other victims reported him and I guess someone believed them.

Years later, when I decided I wanted to go deep within and heal myself, I realized my experience with this loser man had put me into a different type of competition with men. I was already in one in terms of value in society, but this man caused me to build a wall around my heart.

My way of dealing with all my life trauma was not to resent it, but to look for the learning lesson while I was also moving forward, continuing to create, continuing to expand and follow my dreams. But I arrived at a point where I realized I had not let some love into my life due to this incident. I decided to reclaim myself and my heart's capacity to love as I choose, and to do this I realized I needed to take my power back and I did. I healed myself. I performed my own soul retrieval.

When "other" people find out about "your" trauma story, often their only response is "you must forgive the other person!" It's like a compulsion certain people have, specifically people who respond to other societal control mechanisms that are about placing our power outside of ourselves. Real healing is about reclaiming your power within, it's not all about doing something about the other person. So forgiveness is not like what "other" people say at all, in my experience.

For me, I had to forgive myself for seeing what was going to happen and to not be able to stop it. As psychics, we often blame ourselves for getting hurt: "I should have seen it coming." But we are also part human, and that human part of the hurt is something we were meant to go through for a reason. My Soul had a reason. So I had to forgive myself for judging myself and to even uplevel my perspective, as someone helped me do later: they helped me see I'd actually made a heroic effort towards the other kids, done out of love.

I allowed myself to forgive myself, to take back my power from that man and because I loved myself enough to do this, more magic doors opened. The process looked like this:

I confronted him in meditation, and because I was unafraid to see my own weakness, I was able to see his childhood and what happened to him and why he did these things to others. I was able to see that he was going to die soon in jail, and I was able to release our bond. In that way, I forgave him, not in the way church tells you to do it, but in the fact that I offered him the opportunity to show me his story.

I also gave back to him all the abuse he gave me and the emotions I felt as a result so he could hold them, face and feel the results of his actions, feel the wounding on an energetic level (which is where everything begins), that was my punishment for him. I threw all this back to him and saw him fall to his knees, crying. Then I took my parts of self back from him, from his energy, from his memories. I took control in the name of love for myself, and in doing this I disarmed him, I forgave myself, and all that charge around this incident dissolved. I freed myself.

Forgiveness in my experience was about actually turning towards myself. I decided I am a worthy, powerful being, a loving person who's valid no matter what that other person tried to demean me into. I decided that what someone else did to me was not who I am. This allowed me to feel so connected to the universe that I accepted I was in fact part of universe, I did in fact have its wisdom and creativity and love within me.

In this way, I stood in the truth of my infinite beauty, fully accepting my power to create change, and the power and capacity of my heart to love, and to realize my power to love was not a weakness.

I saw the depravity of the other human being and did not take responsibility for his perversion but fully saw his perversion as his own creation, separate from me. I gave him back his creation and took my energy back from him.

In this way I broke myself free from being a victim, and I was rewarded with clarity among many other things that were already mine to have and to be.

CONTINUITY

When I was a very small child, pre-kindergarten years, we would occasionally take family drives to uncle Joe's house.

I have disliked family gatherings since my very beginnings on this planet. In my childhood I didn't feel like a child-I felt like an adult, I was very aware of having been a man before, and I found my small female body very weird and it eventually became a problem for me when I learned how tempting it was for people to treat it badly. But mostly, my reason for not liking family gatherings was that I understood what adults were talking about and I wanted to contribute to the conversations. I didn't understand why adults didn't want me part of their discussions.

But uncle Joe was different. He didn't talk to me, just smiled warmly, and he played music. So when we'd visit, I avoided all the relatives or spent time in the bathroom except when uncle Joe played his music: guitar or harpsichord, it was a safe space when the music was being made. He was tall, thin, black hair and dark eyes. Calm and quiet. I don't have any memories of his voice, just his presence.

Then one day, we were all gathering in the car to go see uncle Joe. Everyone was really sad, the adults were crying, and I didn't know why, because Uncle Joe was in the car with us, and he was warmly smiling at me as he usually did.

I had never ridden in a car with uncle Joe before, and it was nice. So I didn't understand why people were sad, until we arrived at his funeral. I can't say it all made much sense for me at that age: I was aware uncle Joe was still alive, he was right next to me. And still, people were sad and crying and didn't seem to notice he was with us.

Uncle Joe would visit me 30 something years later, one afternoon during a life change that was hugely emotional and scary. At this time I laid down to try and grab just 10 minutes of rest. As I closed my eyes, I felt the need to open them again, and as I did I saw uncle Joe, who didn't speak and yet reassured me that all would be ok. I felt a great sense of calm come over me as he did.

=

As a small child I was always thinking about life and life after death, and this subject would continue to be the one I thought about most often, along with healing, well into my teenage years. I didn't really understand how to add ghosts into this mix, because for me, they were living people still just not as physically touchable.

I thought often about reincarnation, sitting alone in my bedroom, but I wasn't sure how it took place, technically. Since my mind couldn't decide if this was true or not, I left this idea open and felt free to decide at a later date. I'd often revisit it, play around with it in my mind, examined it from all the angles I was able, then I'd put it on my mental shelf, and return later, again and again.

I was I was skeptical about past lives also until I started to experience mine, dozens of them. I started recognizing people in this life that I remembered from past lives. Sometimes they would remember too, and we'd share our memories. I'm sometimes able to take people to their past lives. Sometimes I would have premonitions about people I was about to meet, and the Voice would tell me to carefully proceed, because these meetings are usually full of synchronicity, memories and emotions.

I spent many nights of my childhood escaping the ghosts in my room by running to the bathroom and locking the door, turning on the light and sitting there on the toilet, staring at the ceiling or the art deco wallpaper asking, "Is this real? Am I real or and I dreaming myself alive here right now? Am I alive somewhere else?"

A funny thing happens when you learn about things you naturally know- a bit of separation (or perceived separation) must take place. In order for anything to be "otherness" and not a part of you, this is necessary. So it's like unlearning what you already have learned so you can remember you know it by going through an experience that makes you think you're going into the unknown. In this way, the knowledge you gain (or rather, remember) by going through the experience becomes imbedded fully and naturally in your belief system as a result of your experience.

So if you want to know yourself, usually you go through a challenge (breakup, heartache, health issue, trauma) that separates you from yourself. It's our way of "zeroing out" so you can start to "rebuild", but what you're really doing is rebuilding your understanding of things that you already know through being a mini version of the Universe.

www.ingramcontent.com/pod-product-compliance
Lightning Source LLC
Chambersburg PA
CBHW072337300426
44109CB00042B/1652